Love to Insult

Love to Insult

EDWARD WILSON

authorHOUSE®

AuthorHouse™ UK
1663 Liberty Drive
Bloomington, IN 47403 USA
www.authorhouse.co.uk
Phone: 0800.197.4150

Published by AuthorHouse 10/05/2015

ISBN: 978-1-5049-9197-1 (sc)
ISBN: 978-1-5049-9198-8 (hc)
ISBN: 978-1-5049-9199-5 (e)

A festering odour at the start of the week,
and new and exciting odours I will seek.
To see if it smell as good as I do,
as I try to discover a smell that is new.
A smell that makes the dumb shout,
a smell that not only hangs about.
But a smell that gets into your nose and hair,
is the smell that follows me everywhere.
With breath that can melt iron and steel,
a deadly weapon that I try to conceal.
Brushing my teeth with a toilet brush,
my favourite past time is rolling in dust.
Eating cockroaches is my favourite food,
crunchy with soft centres they taste good.
I know that I can only be what I am,
a tomcat that pretends to be a man.
Spreading toxic gases as I talk,
and making the cripple want to walk.
There is nothing that smells as good as me,
and I am telling you the truth honestly.
Bow here we are at the end of the week,
the soap and water I never bothered to seek.
When I go to the shops, soap I will see,
but how do I use it, can anyone tell me.

Edward Wilson

A gently breeze and there is snow in the air,
yes my friend the winter season is here.
The leaves that are blowing from the trees,
being carried away on the winter breeze.
The birds fly south to where it is warm,
avoiding cold weather and winter storms.
Children playing in the streets,
enjoying the cold winter heat.
Making snowballs to throw at each other,
and to make a snowman they come together.
A carrot for a nose and coal for eyes,
not too big, but just the right size.
The children are happy playing all day,
until the daylight hours fade away.
Then inside to eat and sleep,
a joyful sleep that is very deep.

A group that is as ignorant as the day is long,
if there were a third world war they would live on.
Feasting on cats, dogs, rats and cockroaches too,
too survive there is nothing they would not do.
Eating the remains of a human being,
it will not be believed until it is seen.
A powerful force of ignorance,
thinking that they are Heaven sent.
But God has nothing to do with them,
only pretending to have any friend.
But the reality is different you see,
they think they are better then you or me.
Short on personality and short on charm,
not spreading peace but causing harm.
Like a virus they go invading,
turning the world into a dustbin.
But in all this there is a tomcat,
that is chasing all the rats.
Hiding his smell in a dustbin,
with all the rubbish that is within.

A heart that melts whenever he is near,
a tender moment that lovers secretly share.
A leave that rustles in the wind,
a look of love showing everything.
The joy in your heart and love in your eyes,
and all those feeling of love that she hides.
The ticking of a clock on a wall,
a child bouncing a football.
The things that you never noticed before,
things that make you love him more.
All this happens as he walks into the room,
as your heart jumps and you feel no more gloom.
The things we do not see that are there,
we see them when our loved ones are near

A lady full of charm and grace,
Tina is much more then a pretty face.
A lady full of compassion and desire,
Tina will set your heart on fire.
A lady that is ready to help those in need,
and those that are hungry she would feed.
A lady with a heart of pure gold,
a warming sight to the cold.
A lady, a wife and a mother too,
Tina I know your family loves you.
Last to bed and first to rise,
you are the apple of their eyes.
Tina you are a lady it is true,
and thank you for being you.

Edward Wilson

A tomcat and an orang-utan had a meeting today,
the tomcat hissed a lot before going away.
The orang-utan displayed anger too,
displays of unhappiness between these two.
The satanist that is trying to take over,
to support his movement, he calls another.
To bring him down to his own level,
the satanist is the son of the devil.
The satanist has his minions at his side,
working from the shadows where they hide.
Overthrowing those that the satanist dislikes,
forcing these people to get on their bikes.
But with no true plan for him to follow,
the satanist approach is truly hollow.
Hollow words and hollow acts,
all he does is get on peoples backs.
But his end will come soon, I am sure,
and he will continue with his plans no more.

A winter chill is in the air,
but there is no frost anywhere.
Clouds of white fill the sky,
as the wind gently blows them by.
As the morning sun starts to rise,
as clouds turn orange in the skies.
The grass in the fields are green,
the air is cold but it is clean.
The feeling of winter is all around,
as the wind blows leaves to the ground.
As the sun rises the day gets hotter,
on this day you will need lots of water.
This is the hottest day of the year,
and being sunburnt is my biggest fear.

A winter wind blows down a winter lane,
as from the winter sky falls winter rain.
As summer leaves fall from the summer trees,
being helped by a strong winter breeze.
As snow also starts to fall on this winter's night,
as the temperature drops under the moonlight.
The winter leaves are being blown all around,
as they are being blown towards the ground.
The winter leaves are covered by snow,
after the snow melts the leave will show.
The winter clouds are blown through the night,
in search of the clouds of the daylight.
The clouds sometimes block the moonlight,
as the clouds are blown left to right.
Shadows form on the ground,
as the clouds move all around.
As the clouds block the moonlight,
making shadows in the night.

A winter's morning romance and love is in the air,
as we tenderly and softly hold each other near.
The wind outside is blowing cold,
we feel the heat of love as we hold.
We slowly drift into a dream state,
the love in our hearts can no longer wait.
The moment has come for us to be one,
as the magic of our love has now began.
Hearing the magic all around,
as our love starts to slow down.
In the heat of love we start to glow,
lost in love; our feeling we show.
The heat rises from you and me,
as our hearts truly run free.
The fire in our heart is burning strong,
giving us the desire to carry on.
Lost in the mood hours seem like minutes,
we know that our love perfectly fits.
So we hold each other and fall asleep,
knowing our love we will again repeat.

Edward Wilson

A winter's night that follows after a summer's day,
strong winds blowing the rain clouds away.
As the strong wind blows through the night,
pushing the rain until the daylight.
The trees that are swaying in the wind,
in the early hours of the morning.
The night clouds changing from dark to light,
all of this is done in plain sight.
Nothing is hidden from the eyes of man,
yet people do not truly understand.
the true nature of how the world spins,
or how nature covers all these things.
Twenty-four hours make up one day,
as that day gets under way.

About five foot tall and swinging through the racking,
you are health and safety but it is the piss you are taking.
Walking around like a human thinking that you fit in,
as a tree dwelling primate this is a battle you can not win.
It is rumoured that you are related to King Kong,
as his illegitimate offspring, you came and he had gong.
I guest the responsibly of having an orang-utan near,
was too much for King Kong and this is clear.
Because the day that you were born King Kong left town,
and you were brought up in a circus with no parents around.
You were shown how to walk on two legs,
and each night for your dinner you had to beg.
Bus as the circus went through Romford and you got away,
escaping quietly after the last show at the end of the day.
Because you walk around on two legs and shown how to behave,
but in the circus they never showed you how to shave.
But you learned how to shave so you try to fit in,
and so your new life imitating humans begins.

About five foot tall and a heart of solid gold,
with a personality to match so I am told.
A welcome smile each and everyday,
with never a nasty word will you say.
You try your best to do what is right,
to create a future that is happy and bright.
Your job is hard, like swimming in honey,
you do not do the job only for the money.
But you do your job the best you can,
helping those that do not understand.
Trying hard to show a better way,
hoping that your efforts will pay off one day.
But it is like swimming in honey up hill,
doing your best because you have a strong will.

All these lonely nights led to lonely days,
wishing that these nights would go away.
Waking up with no one in my arms,
and not sharing anybody's charm.
Feeling the loneliness in my heart,
this loneliness is tearing me apart.
Looking at the sky of the morning,
knowing that my heart is yearning.
For someone that I can call my own,
someone that will share my home.
Someone that will share with me,
a future that will end happily.
Someone to share the rest of my life,
someone that will become my wife.
Is she around the corner, I do not know?
so around that corner I must go.

Edward Wilson

All this pain that I feel in my heart,
is slowly tearing our love apart.
Everything that you said to me,
shot me down but also set me free.
You pretend that it is nothing at all,
but the walls of love have started to fall.
You have no idea how I really feel,
or that the pain I feel is real.
So you carry on like nothing is wrong,
even if it feels like our love is gone.
The light of my love is fading fast,
I do not know how love it will last.
There is no anger, only pain,
that goes over in my head again.
Repeating those words more and more,
each time hurting more then before.
Will this love die, I really do not know,
maybe with time my feeling will grow.
But at the moment I have no idea,
because our future is no longer clear.

An orang-utan and a tomcat two worlds apart,
locked in mortal combat to win a dog's heart.
The orang-utan can offer bananas and a tree,
while the tomcat lets his body odour runs free.
The orang-utan offers shelter in the leaves,
the tomcat is irresistible or so he believes.
The tomcat has marked the dog as his own,
trying to take her to a cardboard box that is his home.
But is all this the dog is confused,
for most of her life she has been used.
By people that say I love you,
but their heart is not true.
The decision is your what do you want to do?
a tomcat or an orang-utan it is up to you.

Animal moving all around me every working day,
communicating in they own special way.
Dogs barking to each other as cats meow,
to understand these animals, can you tell me how?
Some dogs behaving like they were cats,
and some behaving like they are rats.
Pursuing a life style other then a human being,
being human they do not know what it means.
Snakes in the grass moving to and fro,
in silences they come, in silence they go.
Seeking problems as they move through the grass,
thinking their authority is going to last.
Then there is the vampire bat looking for prey,
looking for a new victim everyday.
These are some of the characteristics people display,
so look out for them and try to have a nice day.

As children I always looked up to you,
now we are grown I still respect you.
Life is a game of cards that we play,
we try to be the ace with every new day.
We try to avoid being the joker of the pack,
do not take life serious but never slack.
Keeping a balance in all that we do,
you are my role model and I thank you.
We are growing older but not growing apart,
we were born as brother from our very start.
We are no longer babies but you never think twice,
about still giving your baby brother some advice.

Edward Wilson

As darkness falls and the moon is full,
there is a tomcat that is full off bull.
In London's night life he thinks he is a hit,
but in reality he is really just full of _ _ _ _.
Fumigating the night clubs that you go to,
the RSPCA do not want to go anywhere near you.
Your odour is worst then smelly old fish,
for you to go away is the people's wish.
But you are really to stupid to take the hint,
and you think that your breath smells like mint.
He has a smell that even a mother can not love,
when he come near, see gives him a kick and shove.
She would change the locks and shut the door,
and pretend that is does not know him anymore.

As the clock ticks and time goes by,
the older you get the more time will fly.
But will you age with graceful style,
and accept old age with a smile.
Or will you try to hang on to your youth,
hanging on with nail and tooth.
Parading yourself like you are young again,
trying to fit in and make younger friends.
You are unaware that the jokes on you,
and deep down knowing that you are not true.
Lying to yourself and living in the past,
you want those days of yesteryear to last.
But as you reach ninety and your hair falls out,
and you ask yourself what was it all about.
No more living in dreams and accepting reality,
then it will be time to set your mind free.

As the cold winter wind blows across the land,
a wind so strong you will find it hard to stand.
There is a nasty smell carried on this wind,
it is carried for miles as you will find.
The smell is coming from a tomcat,
who in a tree he quietly and calmly sat.
Raising his arms to let the smell out,
as the wind carried it all about.
From the east far and far to the west,
distracting flies and other pests.
Marking his territory for those to smell,
as humans all scream "What the hell.".
Where the smell came from, they are unaware,
weather it is far away or it is very near.
Because it is being carried on the wind,
this hostile smell they will never find.

As the cool wind blows on this hot summer day,
I wish the summer sun would go away.
To let the winter come back once again,
because the winter is like an old friend.
The hotter the day, the more uncomfortable I feel,
and this sweat falling from my body is very real.
But I wear lots of clothes to help me lose weight,
but it leaves me in a wet and smelly state.
But it is ok; I do not need to impress anyone,
I just need to stay out of the hot summer sun.
Waiting for the winter days to get here,
and the cool winter weather everywhere.

Edward Wilson

As the darkness fall across the land,
and it is bedtime for the orang-utan.
Dreaming about King Kong once more,
wishing that King Kong would knock his door.
Saying to me that daddy's home,
my little orang-utan you are not alone.
You are not my only illegitimate child,
having brothers and sister will drive me wild.
Because I will know there are more like me,
trying to set orang-utan kind free.
The son of a king that makes me a prince,
but in times of hardship I still feel the pinch.
All the crown jewels my father took to the porn shop,
to build his empire and trying to get to the top.
But as far as he got he never fulfilled his desire,
which was to have the ability to create fire.
As the alarm bell rings and I get out of bed,
with fragments of my dream still in my head.
The day will come when my dreams will come true,
so to King Kong my father I will always love you.

As the morning sun rises in your smile,
you are asleep, but you sleep with style.
You are my Wrndling and you are my wife,
and I will love you for the rest of my life.
You are a vision and a dream come true,
that is why I will spend my life loving you.
As the years go by and you are getting old,
as you get fat and there is more of you to hold.
There is more to love and more to kiss,
weather you are fat or not you are my happiness.
I rush to work in the morning to rush home to you,
to help you cooking dinner is what I want to do.
When our daughter gets home from working all day,
you calm her down with the attention that you pay.
To her needs and making the family whole,
holding our family together is your goal.

So accept the love of those that love you,
with a love that will always be true.
We have been married more then twenty years,
we have shared our love and all our fears.

Edward Wilson

As the old year is ending and the New Year begins,
take your bad habits and throw them in the bin.
Try to make this year better then before,
make yourself happy by giving more.
Leave behind all that you do not need,
change your goal so you can succeed.
No more bad habits that drive you,
no more heartache, just try to be true.
With less then twenty four hours to go,
will there be rain or will there be snow.
Do not let this stop you from making plans,
because your future rests in your hands.
So a happy New Year to everyone,
may this year be filled with joy and fun.

As the rain falls washing my tears away,
I thought that in my heart you would stay.
But as the rain-washes tears from my eyes,
I now know that our love was a lie.
My dreams of you lived in my head,
now my dreams of you are all now dead.
You broke my heart when you said goodbye,
that was the day that my heart started to die.
Now my world is slowly burning down,
my heart beats softly making little sound.
My little world was built around you,
as this world ended with my love for you.

As the snow falls gently to the ground,
covering everything without a sound.
The wind is blowing down the street,
colder and colder taking away the heat.
As the night goes now and it snows more,
it is safer to stay behind locked doors.
Where you may be protected from the icy wind,
and the ice-cold snow that is falling.
The moonlight is shining down,
as the snow covers all around.
The houses, the cars and the streetlights,
it seems that it is set to snow all night.
So you will wake up to a world of white,
because it snowed all through the night.

As the sun rises early from the east,
a tomcat releases his inner beast.
A odour that can totally kill a fly,
knocking it right out of the sky.
Lifting his arms to let more smell out,
as in horror all those around him shout.
The smell lingers where he has been,
because this tomcat is never clean.
A nasty odour follows him everywhere,
that smells like him so he does not care.
But if you can smell yourself, then you smell,
and you will be known as the smell from hell.
Water is everywhere and soap is cheap,
so why does he smell like a dung heap?
Organic fertiliser of the worst kind,
is the deposit that his body leaves behind.

Edward Wilson

As you walk around, your ponytail will bounce,
filled with venom down to the last ounce.
Your smell is a warning for others to stay away,
the look in your eyes keeps people at bay.
Your breath will paralyse those that come near,
after you captivate them with your hypnotic steer.
Then you will slowly move in for the kill,
while your prey is dazed and quite still.
Then your body odour slaps them in the face,
coming to their senses they leave that place.
Facing the ground and running like mad,
because if you catch them, it will be bad.
So you try another way to get what you need,
biting your lip and into the water supply you bleed.
Blood so toxic, it glows in the dark,
as you poison just one lake in the park.
As the fishes all float to the surface dead,
you eat your dinner then you go to bed.
This is something that I must confess,
this is a tomcat at his very best.

Being shown health and safety by an orang-utan,
is something that I will never truly understand.
A tree dwelling primate teaching a human being,
what has the world come to and what does it all mean.
The world is out of focus and is a funny shape,
with human resources being run by an ape.
An orang-utan and an ape working as one,
where did we go wrong and what have we done.
Scientist are trying to correct the mistake,
the one that the governments seem to make.
To take control back it will take a strong hand,
from someone stronger then an orang-utan.

Blinded by the light and feeling kind of numb;
in a state of confusion and somewhat dumb.
How did this happen, how did I get here,
how was total destruction so very near.
I believed that you were the one for me,
but now I am left in complete misery.
I wanted to believe that all was right,
but you turned out to be a thief in the night.
Now I have lost everything that was mine,
you broke my heart and left me behind.
Now all that is left is an empty shell,
and you have made my life a living hell.

Can you smell it coming in the air tonight?
a strong odour that does not smell right.
A smell that lingers for hours at a time,
I must know that smell I must find.
Then use bleach to make it go away,
but will bleach keep the smell at bay?
I must try, but first I have to get near,
as that nasty smell is hovering here.
The smell is coming from a tomcat,
who at this moment is eating a rat.
Is he aware of my coming I am not sure?
but I have not enough bleach, I need more.
So I tip toe away to get what I need,
about ten gallons of bleach to succeed.

Can you smell that decaying odour in the air?
it means that the tomcat is very near.
The odour that you can cut with a knife,
means that you better start running for your life.
If your have asthma it is time for you to go,
because that smell will bring you down low.
Decaying vegetables and rotting flesh,
this smell is anything but fresh.
This is how the tomcat normally smells,
it is enough to make satan leave hell.
He gets into a bath and the water start fizzing,
the soap evaporates before he starts washing.
No woman would touch him with a ten-foot pole,
so he lay in rubbish and around in it he rolls.

Caught up in a love war that is not going very well,
between cool hand Luke and the gob from hell.
All the other rodents have fallen into line,
even the orang-utan and the tomcat are doing fine.
The baboon at the moment is taking a back seat,
while this love war generates great heat.
Is cool hand Luke stronger then the gob from hell,
will cool hand Luke lose, only time will tell.
Cool hand Luke is a five-foot rat,
if he could fly he would be a vampire bat.
The baboon imitates the honey monster very well,
and when he asks for his honey, it rings my bell.
The orang-utan is feeling left out of all this,
but for some reason, it brings him happiness.
I guess that he is waiting for everything to fall apart,
and then walk in and steal my confused heart.
All this attention that I am getting, will it last?
because I am only a dog of the lowest class.

Close your eyes and relax in the summer heat,
feel the warmth from you head to your feet.
The day is made better because you are here,
my heart beats faster wherever you are near you.
We stand here watching the sea come in,
and the seagull over the sea flying.
Boats in the distance sailing away,
into the sunset and another day.
Feeling the wind blowing on my face,
blowing across the sea leaving no trace.
As the waves crash onto the seashore,
coming closer then the time before.
The sun over the sea begins to set,
the sea touches our feet making them wet.
It is time to leave while there is still light,
as the moon rises at he start of the night.

Closing my eyes and feeling your arms around me,
in your loving arms I feel young and I feel free.
In the wink of an eyes we are many miles away,
in a place where we can be together always.
You are more then a fantasy, a dream come true,
I give all my love and all my heart to you.
If time stood still I want to live in your smile,
but then forever will seem like a little while.
Because time flies when you are having fun,
and I will love you until the dying of earth's sun.
So forever my darling please hold my hand,
as we leave footprints in the sand.
Walking on the beach into the sunset,
these are moments that I will never forget.
As the alarm bell rings and I awake,
these memories in my heart I take.

Edward Wilson

Cry me a river as the tears fall down,
running from your eyes to the ground.
Look into my eyes as your tears fall,
in our relationship I gave you my all.
I gave you my love and I gave my heart,
but you chose to rip my heart apart.
Now I have walked, you realise,
that you were the perfect in my eyes.
But now I have moved on to someone new,
someone that is helping me get over you.
So my me a river, because I no longer care,
because you broke me and treated me unfair.

Did you catch that tomcat that you were waiting for?
no longer waiting on his bed, you have to do more.
You need to bark at him as he meows at you,
a tomcat and a dog together, can this be true.
Your friend the tomcat is playing hard to get,
but does he like other tomcats, I don't know yet.
Will yours be a match to last forever?
can we beat the odds and stay together.
As a dog that is living with a tomcat,
I will keep you warm with my body fat.
I will shower you with what you need,
I will follow you only if you led,
I think we can make this relationship last,
if we can forget about east other's past.

Do you love me or is all this a lie,
will my heart be happy or will it cry.
Is this like a dream come true?
or will I be drifting away from you.
I think that only time will tell,
if our love survives or goes to hell?
Will our love stand like a brick wall?
or will our love crumble and fall?
The efforts must be made on both sides,
being honest and drop the secrets we hide.
Thinking not off ourselves but off each other,
you are not part of the furniture you are lover.
More then that and for the rest of my life,
I married you and you are my wife.

Do you really only wash once a year?
the smell is more then most can bear.
A child only a mother can love may be true,
only after she has taken soap and water to you.
A foul smell that hovers over you,
smells worst then doing a number two.
The food you consume and sweat out,
makes most people scream and shout.
As they start to run to get away,
but your fleas and lice always stay.
In your hair and on your skin,
wherever you are, they are coming.
They home in on your smell ten miles away,
so you can never really get away.
From these creatures that cal you home,
even if no human loves you, you are not alone.

Edward Wilson

Does he really love me and how can I be sure?
after he gets what he wants, will he kick out the door.
Does he feel what I feel deep in my heart?
or has he been using me from the very start.
As I wake up beside him I truly feel joy,
but does he view me as disposable toy?
Am I blinded by the love I think I feel?
am I trying so hard to make this real.
Am I frightened of being all alone?
I never wanted to be on my own.
So I gladly accept the love of anyone,
unaware of what I have just done.
By placing a sign on my back I am a target,
for pain and sadness also for deep regret.
I will solider on because I know what is best,
so I will not listen to the warnings from the rest.

Dreaming about you holding me tight,
keeping me warm throughout the night.
Feeling your lips touching mine,
moments of happiness we can find.
Drifting away on clouds of light,
floating together all through the night.
Drifting away from the setting of the sun,
where our heart can become one.
Feeling the love that you have for me,
as our two hearts are floating free.
Laying in bed I am happy or so it seems,
until I realise that it was just a dream.

Dreaming of you by day and by night,
wishing that I could hold you tight.
Dreaming of places that we can walk,
and as we walk, about our future we talk.
Feeling your magic all around,
with every movement and every sound.
These feelings of love I do not understand,
or the magic from the touch of your hand.
But I live in these moments of endless joy,
as all my unhappiness you destroy.
Never wanting to stray from you,
Holding on to a dream come true.
Holding on to you for the rest of my life,
holding you forever my darling and wife.

Dust on the floor blowing in the wind,
and the rain is falling covering everything.
The sky is crying because of jealously,
because the sun will shine so brightly.
The clouds supply the sky with tears,
as the sky expresses all its fears.
The winter wind blows the leaves from the trees,
as the winter brings the country to its knees.
The jealous sky and the angry wind,
are trting to make the world freezing.
As the cold winter wind moves in,
and so the sub zero temperatures begin.
The snow falls to add to the freeze,
carried on a cold winter breeze.
The big freeze carries on all night,
gripping the world at morning's first light.

Edward Wilson

Each day my world is closing in on me,
it has got to the stage that it is only you I see.
You live in my head and you live in my heart,
I can feel your heart beating when we are apart.
I want to reach out with a loving heart and take your hand,
but if I exposed you to my feelings you will not understand.
So I walk in silence and at your side be near,
so if you need any help, I will be there.
I want to tell you of all that is in my heart,
but if you knew then your hatred may start.
You may become angry as the sight of me,
but I can never set my love for you free.
So I keep my feelings under wraps and remain a friend,
but in my heart I will love you until my end.

Early in the morning as I listen to the wind blow,
what is it doing; what is it saying, I really do not know.
I watch the wind moving through the trees,
it could be a summer or a winter breeze.
Birds in the morning as they sing,
as the morning wind is blowing.
The world spins slowly as daylight comes around,
as you can hear that early morning sound.
The birds singing as the day becomes light,
and foxes have finished their work for the night.
People are yawning and getting out of bed,
still half asleep and out of their head.
Making their way to the bathroom,
then to the kitchen and pick up a spoon.
Grab a cup making something to drink,
Now feeling awake and able to think.
Feeling ready they go on their way,
ready to face another stressful day.

Early in the morning I listen to the wind blow,
what it is trying to say, I really do not know.
But it blow outside me window very strong,
just as the wind comes, it will be gone.
Where does it come from and where does it go,
the wind is here come rain, fog, shine or snow.
The weather seems to have no effect on the wind,
the wind is always there, as you will find.
Blowing very hard or blowing very gently,
always there but no human eyes can see.
The wind as it blows passed your face,
coming and going without a trace.
Is the wind your friend, I think so,
it blows away the rain and the snow.
When you are hot it cools you down,
and it sweeps the litter on the ground.

Early in the morning I look towards the sky,
watching the clouds flowing slowly by.
Listening to the birds as they softly sing,
asking myself what this day will bring.
Also listening to you as you are fast asleep,
as you breathe slowly but also deep.
The morning light shines through the window,
and the daylight world begins to show.
The wind is moving through the trees,
the flowers sway in the gently breeze.
The morning dew on the ground,
also on everything else around.
As the sunrises so does the heat,
filling the homes and the streets.
Making it a very pleasant day,
even if rain is on its way.

Edward Wilson

Escaping from the circus was the easy part,
but pretending to be human, where do I start.
Shaving my face and not walking on all fours,
this is a good start, but there is much more.
I listen to James Brown because he sings to my soul,
if I can sing like him, I will be closer to my goal.
No more swinging through the trees to get around,
but driving a car with four wheels on the ground.
But first I must pass something called a driving test,
to fit in with these humans I will do my best.
I will get a job working on a construction site,
so I can swing through the rafters late at night.
Then leave that job and work in health and safety,
and maybe the humans will start to respect me.
It is not going to easy for me to pass for a human,
because I am the son of King Kong an orang-utan.

Facing toward the rising sun in a dark sky,
as a smelly tomcat sleeps the hours by.
Dreaming of places where he can fit in,
a place where washing in a very big sin.
A place where women drop at my feet,
a place where my body odour smells sweet.
A place where I no one brushes their teeth,
a place where everyone has only one set of brief.
A place where cockroaches can run free,
just like the cockroaches that sleep with me.
A place where drains are allowed to over flow,
a place where dirty sock sometimes goes.
A place where septic tanks overflow,
a place like this, do you know?
I have searched for this place my life long,
but if it did exist, now it is gone.

From being a character in a video game to real life,
from being Donkey Kong to taking a human wife.
You are royalty the son of King Kong,
in you his legacy will carry on.
You are an orang-utan of the highest order,
even thou were abandoned by you father and mother.
You were trained to act human at London zoo,
they somehow managed to get you talking too.
Watching television and you dad on the Empire State,
makes you very happy because you feel great.
How you managed to get a driving license is beyond me,
when all you do in your spare time is climb trees.
But you did it and now you have found work,
a tree dwelling primate and a complete jerk.
You may appear to be human but you can not hide,
the fact that you are an orang-utan deep inside.
You may pretend to be human with a certain style,
but late at night you still hear the calls of the wild.

Get out of that tree King Louie, you are an orang-utan,
a tree dwelling primate that pretends to be a man.
Swinging through the racking when no one is around,
makes you happier then walking on the ground.
Scraping your knuckles on the ground as you walk,
eating with your finger and not using a knife and fork.
Never forgetting that you are King Kong's son,
all you want to do is to have a little fun.
Hanging upside down with bananas in your mouth,
and in the winter months you try to head south.
Some place where it is warm to work on a tan,
remember that you are not human but an orang-utan.

Edward Wilson

Getting up in the morning and washing your body and face,
the whole world over these things are common place.
Getting home from work and having a wash or a bath,
gets rid of those odours of the day at least by half.
Sitting down and eating with someone dear,
shearing tender moments holding them near.
This may apply to all but never to a tomcat,
who comes home from work and in the corner sat.
There are no creature comforts that he seeks,
he only wants to smell like a freak.
Going to sleep in the clothes that he works in,
and in the same clothes his working day begins.
With great difficult brushes his hair,
as the fleas leave and jump everywhere.
No mouthwash and no toothpaste,
he rushes of to work with great haste.
This is how the tomcat's day works out,
and this is what this tomcat is all about.

Give me the morning and give me the night,
stay with me from daylight to daylight.
Feel the beating of my loving heart,
I still feel your heartbeat when we are apart.
The nights are cold when you are not there,
the day seems longer when you are not near.
I carry on trying to find a way,
a way back to your heart to stay.
So I dream a little dream and tell a little lie,
Whatever helps my days to go by.
The day travel faster because I am now asleep,
but in my dreams I have your heart to keep.

Give me the night so I can be near you,
wishing my dreams all come true.
Wishing on the nearest star to me,
wishing that our love can run free.
Looking towards the stars of the night,
wishing that you were here in the daylight.
My dreams seem to holds me together,
in my dreams I love you forever.
So I stay asleep and with you,
this is all that I want to do.
To live with you in my life,
in my dreams you are my wife.
So I close my eyes and drift away,
towards your love and that special day.
The day that we will be joined together,
the day that I will love you forever.
The day we will become one,
the day that my dreaming is done.

Goodbye King Louis as into the sunset you swing,
into the morning as you hear the birds sing.
You left the cars by the park and travelled in the trees,
swinging so fast that you created a breeze.
Avoiding traffic jams by swinging through the night,
and reaching your destination by early morning light.
Back to the jungle and to King Kong's side,
father and son standing together with pride.
Telling King Kong about all you have done,
proving that you never left the jungle to have fun.
You passed your driving test and worked in HR,
and you even when as far as buying two cars.
But you left all those things behind you,
as heir to King Kong this is what you must do.
Stand with pride and take your place,
as into Ape Mountain they carve your face.
The image is placed beside King Kong's,
so the legacy of your father will carry on.

Edward Wilson

He is a tomcat and he is the last of his kind,
a smellier tomcat you will never find.
He special aroma that makes people cry,
he never washes on any day that ends with a Y.
A silent killer of plants and trees,
a funky odour that is carried on the breeze.
Heavier then air so it rests on the ground,
killing flowers and plants all around.
Dogs in his path run for cover,
and babies in prams cry for mother.
Is he unaware of the odours that he brings?
as his body odour is destroying everything.
A smell like nothing that came before,
with each day his smell grows more.
Stronger and stronger day by day,
please smelly tomcat just go away.

Here in the gutter is where I stay,
but I venture out to work some days.
But when I am at home I roll around,
in all the rubbish that is on the ground.
To improve my body odour that smell sweet,
from the top of my head down to my feet.
Making all those around avoid me,
they smell me coming before me they see.
But it is all right and it is part of a plan,
that one day will make me the man.
Creeping through bushes late at night,
once and a while getting into a fight.
Singing out loud to the moon,
knowing that it will be daylight soon.
I know I am special and that is that,
never washing I am a tomcat.
Smelling the roses only if they survive,
my body odour never leaves them alive.

Here in the jungle there is a ruling class,
I will tell you who it is, so there is no need to ask.
Kong is the king of all he surveys,
standing tall from day to day.
But there is a shameful moment from his past,
and the horror of many years ago seems to last.
He fathered a child an orang-utan,
and to hide his shame King Kong just ran.
Hiding out in the jungle for days,
hoping that this problem would go away.
A orang-utan with royal blood in his veins,
for many years has caused King Kong great pain.
Chased out of the jungle and all alone,
the orang-utan made a circus his home.
Travelling the world he finally got away,
roaming the streets of London night and day.
,Standing on two legs and learning to talk,
no more swinging through tree, but trying to walk.
Now the orang-utan works as health and safety,
and from the orang-utan King Kong is finally free.

Here in the morning with the lights in the sky,
with plenty of activity happening on high.
The stars are shining, up in the sky,
as aeroplanes go flying slowly by.
The streetlights are flickering off and on,
as power to the streetlights will soon be gone.
The morning clouds are gathering overhead,
while I am still asleep in my warm bed.
The sunlight filters through the clouds,
as the clouds seem to form a shroud.
Covering the world in shades of white,
softly filtering the strong sunlight.

Edward Wilson

Hiding Responsibility is what HR really do,
Hopelessly Retarded applies to them too.
In reality they really are company glove puppets,
but on whom hand do they really sit.
Who is the person that pulls their strings?
who makes them dance, who makes them sing.
Walking around in shirts and ties,
too be helpful, they never try.
Highly Responsive they are not,
they would rather leave you to rot.
Hungry Rats more fit the bill,
as mindless zombies with no will.
HR are required by the law,
HR in name but no more.

Hold me in the morning and hold me in the night,
whenever you hold me in your arms the world seem right.
Look into my eyes as my heart drifts away,
into your hands where it will forever stay.
These feeling that I have for you in my heart,
keep me warm whenever we are apart.
These tender moments that we share together,
I want to live in them, to make them last forever.
The years go by in the twinkling of an eye,
but our love for each other will never die.
So hold me forever and our future we will see,
as we remain in love for all eternity.

Human resources but how can this be,
more like brainless morons in a tree.
Human resources a group that shares a brain,
and from doing the right thing they reframe.
Human resources ignorant to the end,
driving others crazy and around the bend,
Human resources useless to the last drop,
how do we get their madness to stop?
Human resources the most dump of all,
their madness will drive you up the wall.
Human resources in name alone,
but they really have heads of bone.
If you encounter human resources beware,
they are really stupid and not all there.

I am a cross between an orang-utan and a human being,
as I ponder my life trying to find out what it all means.
Was I created by nature or in a laboratory?
all these questions are far too many for me.
If I was created in a laboratory, what of King Kong,
my search for answers gives me the strength to go on.
The answers of my origin and how I came to be,
were lost when green peace came and rescued me.
Now all I know is that I was a government experiment,
but what is the purpose of my creation and what it all meant.
Was I an accident of scientists gone mad?
or am I the left over of something really bad.
I am prince orang-utan the son of King Kong,
and my mother was a test tube, but sadly has gone.
So I am left knowing that I created out of wedlock,
I am a scientific experiment but not to me mocked,

Edward Wilson

I am caught in a trap and do not know what to do,
I am in love with a tomcat, a baboon and an orang-utan too.
The baboon and the orang-utan have a similar style,
the tomcat's body odour really drives me completely wild.
The orang-utan really loves his nuts,
the baboon lives in a semi-detached hut.
The tomcat sleeps in the corner of a room,
his dreams of me makes his heart zoom.
Is it mating season, is it that time of year?
I am real easy and I do not really care.
I am just your average loveable dog,
and every night I sleep like a log.
My hair is shading, so you know where I have been,
the tomcat walk behind and my mess he will clean.
The orang-utan wants to give me his nuts,
as a means of helping me out of this rut.
He thinks that I am too fat, but that is okay,
because I seem to spreading myself thin these days.
Just when I felt that I was doing very well,
I fell in love with the gob from hell.

I am hanging out in a tree up side down,
watching everything that happens on the ground.
Eating bananas, berries and apple too,
but I want to eat meat like humans do.
But I can not do that because I am an orang-utan,
and I am only playing at being a mortal man.
But I truly love swinging through the trees,
and I love feeling that cool gentle breeze.
Human beings are really missing out,
on what being an orang-utan is all about.
I am King Louie the great orang-utan,
who will never really be a man.

I am here in the cold light of day,
wishing that in your arms I could stay.
Watching you as you slowly move,
my aching head you can soothe.
The times that I have watched you before,
makes me love you more and more.
Your face is incredible and your body too,
I want to spend the rest of my life next to you.
To hold you tight and be your man,
or take you shopping and hold your hand.
For the rest of my life I will love you,
this is what I was born to do.
So I will stand beside you, as we grow old,
and within my heart I have you to hold.

I am in deep confusion and I do not understand,
am I really a human or am I really an orang-utan.
I have many questions and here is another,
if King Kong is my father, then who is my mother?
I have a job that I know nothing about,
but it gives me a reason to get out.
Out of the zoo on a day pass,
but how long will this privilege last?
I must have an escape plan ready to deploy,
thinking about escaping brings me great joy.
But my pass is good for five times a week,
without it my future would look bleak.
But the humans where I work love me,
to see their faces is worth breaking free.
It will be worth it to see them again,
Maybe one day we can be more then friends.

Edward Wilson

I am in love with a dog but he is my teddy bear,
he is money grabbing low life but I do not care.
He is the loving that I need each and everyday,
so by his side each day I will want to stay.
I am his loving lady and he is my loving man,
but recently I got the attention of an orang-utan.
He showers me with bananas while hanging in a tree,
but could this orang-utan really love me?
Or is he looking for a roll in the hay?
if the answer is yes, then just go away.
But also there is a tomcat hanging around,
with his head in the sky and not on the ground.
But I will stay with my dog for he is big and bad,
also if I was to leave him, he will get really mad.

I am King Louie the one and the only,
from King Kong I set myself free.
To create the kingdom that is for me,
and setting up home in my own tree.
My father King Kong would love to shout,
from his kingdom I just had to get out.
Now I am building my own life,
and from the humans I found a wife.
I can not tell my wife of my past,
because I want my marriage to last.
But my father keeps trying to find me,
I am his only son, but I want to be free.
I fit in with the humans and own a car,
in the human world I have come far.
Walking on two legs and learning to smoke,
now making fire seems like a big joke.
It is something I can do everyday,
I strike a match and throw it away.
I moved out of my tree and into a home,
because I am no longer living alone.

I ask myself is it right or is it even fair,
that everyday I want to hold you near.
These feeling that I get when I look at you,
will one day make all my dreams come true.
But for the moment I will sit and wait,
and when the time is right I will not hesitate.
To take you in my arms and take you away,
to where my love grows stronger everyday.
I will wrap you in a love so tender,
as my heart to you I will surrender.
One mind sharing the two hearts,
as we move forward we will never part.

I can feel it all around, yes I can feel it in the air,
I can feel that my one and only true love is here.
I feel the love coming from your heart to me,
as your love gently wraps itself around me.
The feeling that I get from seeing you,
seems like a dream that has come true.
My heart calls your name with each beat,
and your smile knocks me of my feet.
You are perfect in every way,
and I have you in my heart everyday.
When I wake up in the morning, it is you I see,
as you lay there sleeping gently beside me.
You are the best thing in my life,
you are my future and you are my wife.

Edward Wilson

I can feel it coming in the air tonight,
it is your love that will hold me tight.
I feel your love as it gently covers me,
you are my dream and my fantasy.
I hear you travelling on the wind,
this is how my nights always begin.
Then I drift into a world where dreams live,
every night to you my heart I give.
You are the star of my story everyday,
I will hold you in my heart each day.

I close my eyes and see you in my head,
weather I am at work or in my bed.
You live in my heart, but you are unaware,
that I love you and want you always near.
The loving glow that come from your smile,
your gentle personality and graceful style.
You are unaware of what you do to me,
but when you look at me, what do you see?
Do you see a man that is madly in love?
who will fit you just like a velvet glove.
Or do you see someone that is a friend,
someone that will make you smile again.
It is up to you which way you want to go,
but I am here for you and I want you to know.

I close my eyes and visions I see,
visions of your love surrounding me.
I look into my heart and you are there,
so every tender moment we will share.
I close my ears and your heartbeat I hear,
weather you are far away or you are near.
I sit still and I can feel your heartbeat,
I feel it from my head to my feet.
You are my dream and you are my life,
I wish to hold you forever as husband and wife.
This is just the fantasy that I hold in my heart,
we are only friends, well that's how it starts.

I do not know how you get into my bedroom and lick my face,
your breath is truly smelly and it is a true disgrace.
I have tired to get toothpaste for you in the pet shop,
hoping that your truly bad breath will stop.
Your nose is wet showing that your healthy,
as you chase cats around the garden happily.
The tree in the garden is where you mark your spot,
and you roll around in the dirt when you are hot.
You used to like to chase cars and buses too,
but the last time something happened to you.
You slipped on the pavement and hurt your leg,
you limped home and went straight to bed.
I called the vet to make sure that you were all right,
but you were in great pain all of that night.
They took you to the hospital to operator on you,
and they fixed you up as good as new.
Now you just sit around the house getting fat,
to tell the truth I am much happier with that.

Edward Wilson

I dream of sharing my kennel with a dog like you,
so I plan to sell my kennel and move in with you.
The way you rub my tummy and brush my hair,
has fooled me into believing that you care.
When I sell my kennel, you just want my money,
then you will treat me as a joke and think I am funny.
Then you will upset me and throw to a tomcat,
who is really is just a low down nasty rat.
Who never washes or shampoos his hair,
but enjoys sniffing my underwear.
Is this what all rats do in the dark?
sniffing underwear and leaving a mark.
Marking their territory to keep others away,
so later on he can work, rest and play.
Maybe in the future but not right now,
a dog and a tomcat getting together, how?
Maybe scientists can lend a hand,
and one day help me to understand.
How a tomcat and a dog can be together?
and make their relationship last forever?

I drift away into a world off deep sleep,
no longer will I have to count sheep.
as I walk along a calm seashore,
looking at the things I have seen before.
Feeling the wind blowing on my face,
as the sea comes in and out without a trace.
The trees in the background softly sway,
as the sun sets at the end of a beautiful day.
The sky turns orange and then red,
as the sun sinks into the sea and to bed.
Sea birds fly pass the setting sun,
watching crabs as they try to run.
Back into the sea before it goes out for the night,
quickly moving sideways out of my sight.
As the moon comes up in a night blue sky,
I lay on the sand and watch the birds fly by.

I feel in the morning that you are drifting away,
drifting into your dreams and into another day.
Drifting into another time and space,
drifting to a totally different place.
But are you drifting with me by your side,
or is there some other love that you hide.
Where you two meet in your mind,
which will break my heart, it's very unkind.
The shadows of love that are left behind,
no longer a home for them to find.
I am sure that it is all not true,
because of the love I have for you.
But do you have my love in your heart?
are you with someone else when we are apart?
I want to believe that you are here for me,
and my future is not you, me and she.

I feel it in the morning as I lay here in my bed,
I have images and visions running through my head.
I hear voices that call out in the middle of the night,
and while my eyes are open I see flashing lights.
Is this a dream or is this my reality,
all of these things around me that I see.
I feel a fever and I am feeling very hot,
it seems like an infection I have got.
Drinking plenty of hot drinks,
keeping warm until the fever sinks.
Staying in bed and trying to sleep,
the fever under control I must keep.
So I close my eyes and lay my head,
lying fast asleep in a warm bed.

Edward Wilson

I feel the cold in the cold morning air,
passing through me like I was not there.
The aches and pains I have in my head,
started as I lay down on my bed.
The temperature of my body is getting hot,
I will throw my cards in this is my lot.
But am I giving up, not at all,
I will rest until my temperature fall.
I am sweating hard and getting wet,
I know I am not over the worst yet.
The walls close in as daylight fades away,
trying to make it to another day.
Slowly but surely my body will recover,
and a brand new day, I will face another.

I feel the love in the air tonight,
it surrounds me like a glow of light.
It keeps me warm as the wind blows,
it keeps me dry in rain or snow.
I feel the magic of a memory,
of the last time that you were with me.
I hear your voice in the wind,
sweet and softly singing.
I feel your touch in every raindrop,
it makes me sad when it stops.
But I feel your love in all my life,
you are special; you are my wife.

I feel the magic moving through the air,
and the magic I feel in having you near.
I can see the magic in your loving eyes,
as I watch you as the night drifts by.
I feel the magic in the touch of your hand,
this warmth of love I do not understand.
But all of this magic I feel from you,
makes you my only dream come true.
So I will stay by your side for always,
and we will live together everyday.
As our days get darker turning to night,
you are my love and my guiding light.

I feel the morning wind softly on my skin,
I see the affects of the morning wind.
I hear the morning birds as they sing,
I watch the morning sun rising.
I watch the leaves fall from trees,
carried away on the morning breeze.
I watch the morning sky change,
as the morning lights are arranged.
I feel the fresh morning dew,
washing the morning new.
I watch the clouds sink low,
I have watched the rain turn to snow.
All these things I have seen from my birth,
I am not human, but I am mother earth.

Edward Wilson

I found out today that I am the son of King Kong,
when I was first told, I was sure that they were wrong.
King Kong is the greatest in all our land,
and I am nobodies child just an orang-utan.
Raised in a circus and learned walk,
and to form simple word so I can talk.
I tried to learn how to use a knife and a fork,
but for an orang-utan, I looked like a dork.
I passed my driving test in a bumper car,
and now I feel like I am a big star.
But I will never be a big as my father,
but there must be a way, I will find another.
I have found out what my father's true desire,
is one day to have the ability to make fire.
So I have taken steps to achieve this goal,
to be able to make fire, I would sell my soul.

I had a dream that you were in love with me,
in my dream both our hearts were running free.
I held you in my arms and we started to kiss,
and from inside my dream I felt happiness.
In my dream I felt the warmth of your touch,
and in my dream all this proved too much.
In this dream that I had last night,
as we kissed, we held each other tight.
In my dream I did not really care,
because in my dream, you were there.
This dream that I had on my bed,
for days to come stayed in my head.
This dream that I had that I can not share,
because in reality, you are not near.
So the dream of you stays in my heart,
where we can be together and never part.

I know that you do not love me or even care,
there will be no tender moments that we share.
Our relationship died before it actually begun,
You never took me serious, I was just some fun.
I am no one's entertainment or a game to play,
so it is in my best interest to stay well away.
It makes me say but this is what I must do,
so that I can start to get over loving you.
But then you smile at me with a stolen glance,
and my heart leaps and I think I have a chance.
But then you start to laugh and I realise,
I am just a puppet in your scornful eyes.
So hello loneliness and to happiness goodbye,
it is time to forget you; so I will try.

I know why doors are opening for me and I am not wrong,
it is all because I am the illegitimate son of King Kong.
So I can swing through the racking as much as I like,
but no one has showed my how you ride a bile.
But I learned to drive at the circus in a bumper car,
and I knew that this skill would carry me far.
Then I escaped from the circus and stole a bus,
the passengers were screaming and making a fuss.
But I did not crash the bus and the passengers were okay,
then I quickly got out of the driver's sit and ran away.
I am an orang-utan working as Health and safety,
but none of the humans ever listen to me.
So I swing through the racking feeling at home,
even if I am swinging through the racking alone.
There is one thing I love more then climbing trees,
is driving with the top down and feeling the breeze.
Rushing through the hair on my face,
that feeling of joy I can not replace.

Edward Wilson

I lay here in bed with my lovely wife,
she is my future and the love of my life.
She is the one that I come home to,
she lives in my heart and will always be true.
She holds my heart in the palm of her hands,
she is always kind and she understands.
She is perfect in all that she says and do's,
I would surely die if her love I did lose.
So I stay by her side continually,
because her love lives inside me.
I live to love her more each day,
with a love that will never fade away.
So I lay her in bed with my lovely wife,
because she is the most perfect thing in my life.

I lay here in the morning next to you,
knowing that you are my dream come true.
Watching you as you are fast asleep,
listening to you breathing soft and deep.
Watching you as you move in the bed,
wondering what is going on in your head.
The morning light shines through the window,
I am here with my wife; this is all I know.
Feeling the love that you have for me,
even in your sleep, it is plain to see.
Now I have found true happiness in my life,
happy with the fact that you are my wife.

I lay in my bed looking up at the ceiling,
not really sure of what I am feeling.
Just out of hospital and feeling blue,
because I want to be held by you.
The day slowly turns to night,
and I long to hold you tight.
But you are far away with another,
now I know that you are not my lover.
I lay on my bed crying all night,
it hurts so much, this is not right.
No text message and no phone call,
I am so angry, I want to climb the wall.
But I realise that I am better of without you,
and to myself I must always be true.

I look into the morning light after the night before,
watching the sunrise as it beauty shows more and more.
The many colours of the morning in the morning sky,
colours that are reflected on the clouds that float by.
Birds of the morning that fill the morning with song,
singing all through the day until the sun has gone.
The lights of the evening the lights of the setting sun,
these lights have been there since the world begun.
The world that spins is wrapped in light,
from sunrise to sunset and the cold of night.

Edward Wilson

I refuse to accept that I am getting old,
it is a fantasy, or so I am told.
My brain tells me that I am fine,
getting bigger muscles and a firm behind.
My body feels much younger too,
with all the exercising that I do.
Trying to eat food that is good,
eating healthily as we all should.
Getting healthy from the inside out,
and regular exercise is what it is all about.
Drinking plenty of water each day,
and younger looking you will stay.
Your hair going grey is not old age,
but a fashion statement, it is all the rage.
Not getting old, it is a sign of maturity,
it is something that will happen to you and me.

I saw the sun setting in a tired sky,
as a tired wind blew the clouds by.
I hear the water going down the drain,
I hear the impact of the falling rain.
I see the wind blowing through the trees,
I watch the leaves being carried on the breeze.
I see my darling sleeping on her bed,
as she keeps her secrets in her head.
All the things that I see and hear,
and the things with the world I share.
All the things that I feel in my heart,
some of these things can tear me apart.
All these things that make me strong,
so with my life I can carry on.

I sit here with writer's block thinking what to write,
I have been feeling this great blockage all night.
So I take a deep look into my deep heart,
to find a place where my inspiration starts.
I find an image of your loveliness there,
which means that you go with me everywhere.
Then I find the inspiration that I need,
to give this poem the strength to succeed.
So in my heart and in my head,
as we lay on a floating bed.
laying on a cloud of pure love,
listening to rain falling from above.
Feeling the warmth of your loving embrace,
feeling the magic from your smiling face.
No more writer's block or emptiness,
because you have given me back my happiness.

I think you are barking up the wrong tree,
because you love a useless person like me.
I do not love you; it is your money I need,
this is my weakness and this is my greed.
To make you sell your house and give to me,
all your money so that I may be free.
Free from the bills that tie me down,
knocking those huge bills to the ground.
Then like toilet tissue I will throw you away,
and then I will be free to go on my way.
Seeking other women besides you,
and doing what I want to do.
But until then, to you I will be nice,
to get your money I make this sacrifice.

I want to live in a dream by your side,
having a love that can not easily hide.
I want to travel to many places with you,
and everything together we will do.
I want to hold you everyday,
and in your arms forever stay.
I want all these dreams to come true,
because I want to spend my life with you.
I have no lust and I have no desire,
but my love for you is a consuming fire.
The fire of love is burning strong,
giving me the strength to carry on.
Beyond the day that my hair turns grey,
I will love you more with each new day.

I was at home when my doorbell went ding dong,
I open the door to see my long lost father King Kong.
I asked him why is had left me all alone,
and why he had never taken me home.
He replied that he had been watching over me,
he has always been there even if I could not see.
He would sing to me in his heart at night,
and hold me in his mind until daylight.
But tell me father because I have to know,
why suddenly yourself you now show.
My son I am getting old and very grey,
and it will not be long before I pass away,
Do not cry my son make no sound,
for over my kingdom you will be crowned.
So leave this place and come with me,
and your entire kingdom you will see.
Try to walk tall and try to be a man,
even if you are only an orang-utan.
You are of a royal bloodline a G-utan,
this burden fall to you please understand.
For this my wish and your birthright,
to lead orang-utan kind into the light.

I watch you as you sleep at night,
with your little eyes closed tight.
Your sleep is so very peaceful.
like you are wrapped in cotton wool.
You breathe softly throughout the night.
sleeping gently until the daylight.
Your dreams seem peaceful too,
are you dreaming of me and you?
The nights no longer seem to be cold,
because as you sleep I have you to hold.

I watch you from a distance and your style,
the way you walk makes my heart smile.
I listen to your voice as you talk,
it is equally as sweet as your walk.
Your hair is long and lovely but a little grey,
and I dream of holding your hand one-day.
Your eyes are like pools in the moonlight,
and in my desires I am holding you tight.
But my dreams come to me late at night,
but I wake up alone in the daylight.
My dreams are all I have in my heart,
We work in the same place but are miles apart.
Until I get home and I am holding you,
in my dreams that may never come true.

Edward Wilson

I watch you walking through my dreams,
I do not know what all this means.
I do not know how my heart feels,
or are these feeling in my heart real.
Am I lying here in your warm arms?
losing myself in your tender charms.
Drifting away into time and space,
losing myself in your beautiful face.
The magic that comes from your smile,
will drive me crazy in a short while.
I hear my heart whispering to you,
with each heartbeat saying I love you.
feeling you heartbeat against my chest,
as you slowly lay down to rest.
Deeply asleep and drifting through the night,
drifting in a boat of love towards the daylight.

I will buy you some winalott prime,
the dog food you eat all the time.
Please keep chasing sticks in the park,
and stop chasing busses after dark.
The last time you fell and hurt your leg,
I also think that you landed on your head.
Because you have not been the same since that day,
and the bus you were chasing got away.
In all honesty this is not a thrill,
because I am left with a vets bill.
If you were playing and chasing sticks,
you would be healthy and not be sick.
My pet insurance covers you this time,
but you are no longer in your prime.
Your value to me is you are man's best friend,
but next time you are hurt it will be your end.
Your old body can no longer take the abuse,
but as man's best friend you still have some use.
All that will change if you keep messing around,
I will take you to the vets and have you put down.

I wish that I could think like I was a man,
instead of me thinking like an orang-utan.
I rub two sticks together to make fire,
and I try everyday to fulfil this desire.
I am the son of a king true royalty,
a son of King Kong, but I am unhappy.
Why did my father abandon me at birth?
to be with my father I will give the earth.
But he hid his track and I have no idea,
why he avoided having me anywhere near.
Was I a disappointment from the day I was born?
was it the thought of my coming making you yawn?
When I was born you got up and ran away,
and mother has not seen you to this very day.
I am the son of a king and that should comfort me,
but trying to be human, I am out of my tree.

If only I could be free to swing through the trees,
and on my face I could feel the cool breeze.
Blowing through the hair on my face,
moving silently and without a trace.
I am a orang-utan the son of King Kong,
and all those doctors can not be wrong.
Created from King Kong's bodily fluid,
creating a friendly primate was they did.
I am more a pest then anything,
but if you give me some fruit I will sing.
I am the son of King Kong this is true,
but there are humans that I listen too.
These humans gave me a job to do,
and to myself I get to be true.
I swing through the racking everyday,
and my employers think this is okay.
I am the son of King Kong I say with pride,
King Kong abandoned me and now he hides.
Where he is hiding I really do not know,
but when I find him, to his side I will go.

Edward Wilson

If you are as old as you say, come into my arms,
you will feel 48 again and all of my charms.
If you think that life is passing you by,
take my hand and together we can fly.
I am your friend; let me comfort you.
I will try to make you feel brand new.
When life gets too hard for you to take,
I will share your troubles and mistakes.
When darkness fall in the middle of the night,
take my hand as we walk towards the light.
So close you eyes and drift away and see,
what being 48 feels like, come and hold me

If you had two brains you would be twice as stupid,
judging from some of the things that you did.
Selling your house and give the money away,
as you start your journey to cardboard city today.
You wasted your time impressing who you like,
now you have nothing, they tell you on your bike.
Now you are left alone and in the cold,
because you never listened to what you were told.
You never wanted to listen to those that care,
but to those who's treatment toward you was unfair.
You have given everything too fulfil their desire,
now your life has gone up in smoke and fire.
Now those that cared care no more,
because you never listened before.

If you smell me coming in the middle of the night,
then I already have you locked in my sight.
A juicy morsel for me to get my hands on,
then all night we can sing our song.
a lovely feline with hair of darkest black,
and there will be nothing you will lack.
The after-shave that I choose to wear,
essence of tomcat will draw you near.
An after-shave that smells like no other,
is the reason that we are together.
We grow old together with our children here,
and our grandchildren are also near.
This feeling of family in my heart I keep,
but then I wake up from my deep sleep.
Essence of tomcat drove you away,
that is why I am alone today.

In the darkest night there is rain on the floor,
King Louie comes waking through the door.
Scrapping his knuckles along the ground,
then standing on two legs and looking around.
Once a while to be human he pretends,
for him to be human will be a Heaven send.
But King Louie is only an orang-utan,
that only plays at being a man.
Driving around in a second hand car,
from the jungle to London he has come far.
Every time he passes trees he gets homesick,
but trying to be human he must try to stick.
Some times on nights as dark as this,
he swings through the trees, such happiness.
He wants to buy a house with a garden in it,
so he can build a tree house and in it sit.

Edward Wilson

In the darkness and just out of sight,
a nasty odour is coming into the light.
Carrying a virus in his long hair,
spreading infections everywhere.
Breathing on flowers and killing them dead,
as they all fall like balloons of lead.
His tail bouncing as he slowly walks,
breathing out pollution as he talks.
Not really caring who he breathes on,
I can tell you this, his smells very strong.
Decaying matter like rotting flesh,
he thinks these odours smell fresh.
This is a tomcat that does not brush his teeth,
someone please tell him to turn over a new leaf.
If you think he will listen to you,
please tell him what he must do.
Soap and shampoo is what I mean,
so he can wash himself clean.

In the heat of winter in the middle of the night,
Lying in bed holding my lovely wife tight.
The wind outside blows against the window,
blowing the rain and blowing the snow.
The temperature drops and it is cold,
but I have my darling wife to hold.
There is an electric fire burning bright,
creating shadows throughout the night.
The world outside and the cold of night,
searching for the winter daylight.
But the mood is set for lovers everywhere,
with feelings of love for lovers to share.

In the middle of a large still lake,
is a nasty and poisonous snake.
waiting for boats sailing by,
to toss those boats into the sky.
then to devour the people in that boat,
once they fall into the lake, they never get out.
With a tongue that looks like a ponytail,
if you are in the water he will not fail.
To grab you and pull you down,
where death and darkness is all around.
As he strikes you will notice a smell,
about this you may not live to tell.
But on the off chance you get away,
by swimming for your life that day.
So avoiding a nasty and sticky end,
you will never go into the water again.

In the middle of the night snow steadily falls,
as it gathers on the houses, windows and walls.
The night is not silent as you hear the wind,
whispering softly "Do not go out, but stay in".
As the snow falls turning the night white,
of the snow is reflections of the moonlight.
Footprints of foxes looking something to eat,
but they will fight each other if they meet.
Dogs are hiding in homes that are warm,
hiding away from the oncoming storm.
The world at night sleeps away,
throughout the night and into the day.
Look out the window seeing the snow on the ledge,
looking into the garden seeing the snow on the hedge.
Children wake up but do not understand,
why they can not go and make a snowman.
But they must get ready for school,
sorry kids but those are the rules.
But you can have fun on your way,
so you can throw snowballs today.
The joys of winter adults no longer know,
unlike the children that play in the snow.

Edward Wilson

In the midnight hours and shadows are everywhere,
some are still but some move from here to there.
Shadows moving in the wind and some moving on feet,
but in the daylight hours these shadows will re-treat.
Back into the normal lives that they led,
a normal existence that they really need.
Working to cover the bill that they have,
their daylight hours are full of close shaves.
But in the shadow hours you can be what you want to be,
finding new ways to escape and to make yourself free.
So as a shadow I will walk into your heart,
because in the daylight hours we are apart.

In the moonlight in the middle of the rain,
stands a tomcat that is lacking a brain.
Wanting a partner to play in rubbish tips,
and together from a toilet bowl sip.
Finding food where no one else would look,
in places that the other have long ago forsook.
Roaming the streets and we never wash,
a tomcat and his partner in love they are lost.
Singing together in the pale moonlight,
waking sleeping humans all through the night.
Then finding somewhere that we can rest,
as you lay your sleepy head upon my chest.
You do not mind the smell because you smell the same,
To waste time washing that is truly a shame.
Will I find a partner and make a home,
or will I be forever staying here alone.

In the morning I hear the clock ticking,
do I live in your heart or is it wishful thinking.
I watch you as you sleep so gently,
and I wonder if you are dreaming of me.
I listen to you breathe as you sleep,
wondering of the secrets that you keep.
As you sleep I look at your hair,
do I live in your heart, am I there?
Do you remember me when we are apart?
I need to know that I am in your heart.
Do you think of me when I am out of sight?
are you thinking about me as I hold you tight?
I need to feel that your love for me is true,
because with all my aching heart, I love you.

In the of the night as a strong wind blows,
and the streetlights through the branches show.
It is dark and lonely and very cold,
as the strong winter wind takes hold.
The leaves are leaving the winter trees,
carried away by the strong winter breeze.
As a tomcat tries to stay on his feet,
searching for something to eat.
Trying to find himself a rat of a mouse,
then after eating take shelter near a house.
But there is nothing but dry pieces of bread,
which will have to do then he looks for a bed.
Somewhere that he can keep himself warm,
somewhere that he can ride out the storm.
Since he was thrown out of where is called home,
he is now living in cardboard boxes all alone.
He is no longer of any fixed address,
which is another reason his hair is a mess.
No personal grooming just a nasty smell,
but the odour serves him very well.
It paralyses rats while he eats,
and knocks mice of their feet.
So him being thrown out was a good thing,
now he is free to go anywhere and do anything.

Edward Wilson

Is King Kong my father or am I an only child,
if I had any brothers or sister, it will be wild.
It means that I am not in this world alone,
and as royalty not work my fingers to the bone.
I can swing through the racking holding my nuts,
and maybe visit Tarzan and Jane in their hut.
Tarzan's hut is really an office, you see,
as the director's son, he is superior to me.
But if my dad King Kong showed his face,
Tarzan would turn tail and leave this place.
I am not as big or powerful as my dad,
being a slimily little idiot is my bad!
To follow in my father's footstep I will try,
but before I can do that, I am sure I will die.
So I will try to do the best that I can,
after all I am just an orang-utan.

Is this what I have to do to get next to you,
making myself suffer to prove my love is true.
Feeling the pain that you put me through,
all this suffering is because of you.
Working for my daily bread hands and knees,
with my head to the ground so I can not see,
It seems that you want to hurt me more,
inflecting more pain that the time before.
There must be something else that I can do,
to prove that I always be in love with you.
I look to the and I look to the right,
in terrible pain and with fading sight.
Hoping that one day you will see,
all the love that lives inside of me.

It feels like winter and it feels like snow,
and the cold wind blows passed my window.
The night is lonely as darkness falls,
like a wet blanket covering us all.
The moon in the sky giving light,
to a cold and windy winter's night.
The snow is falling gently to the ground,
covering everything as it falls down.
The night is turning the world white,
as the snow falls throughout the night.
The winter wind blows through the trees,
carrying snow flakes on the winter breeze.
The snow is falling harder now,
covering everything with snow.

It has began, you have played your hand,
your ways made clear now I understand.
You are dealing under the table very low,
where your deceit will stop I do not know.
You are playing with fire but are you unaware,
you are trying to destroy a family and do not care.
You are very calm like you have done this before,
your deceit started the moment you got your foot in the door.
But the door is closing and you are being pushed out,
and I know that you will want to scream and shout.
But the damage is done now go your way,
and leave this family alone this very day.

Edward Wilson

It is amazing the things that you can do,
showing your true colours is something new.
Swinging through the trees on your way to work,
some people seem to think that you are a big jerk.
But you are only just an orang-utan,
who is only playing at being a man.
Taking a human wife to be your mate,
but you are King Louie a primate.
Which does not matter to you at all,
you are playing human and having a ball.
From time to rime you let your hair down,
as you scrape your knuckles along the ground.
Not caring who around you will see,
forgetting the lies and setting yourself free.
If you want children you better forget,
you can not spring your young on the world yet.
The world will never accept children from you,
so hiding your young is the only thing to do.
Let your children play in the trees all day,
but as night falls you must lock them away.
To keep them safe from unbelieving eyes,
so you must be ready to tell some lies.
To protect your young and your wife,
telling the same lies for the rest of your life.

It is cold outside and there is a storm brewing,
all this is happening very early in the morning.
Storm clouds are gathering from the south,
it seems like the wind is coming from God's mouth.
The wind is blowing hard and fast,
will it get stronger and will it last?
This storm is like no storm before,
as trees and uprooted more and more.
Hitting houses taking tiles from roofs,
if this is the end of days, I need more proof.
Moving with destruction through the streets,
changing everyone that it meets.
Changing the temperature from hot to cold,
chilling everyone to there very soul.
Those that sleep on the streets at night,
may not live to see a new day's light.
It is morning but there is no daylight,
so it still seems like it is the night.
The storm goes on bringing rain and snow,
will this carry on all night, no one knows.
But as the sun rises and the storm fades away,
showing what seems to be a perfect day.
The storm cleaned the world last night,
to show the beauty of the world in the daylight.

It is early in the morning and the world is dawning,
and my lovely wife is beside me as she is sleeping.
It is very cold as the world slowly turns,
no more summer sun in the sky that burns.
It is the time for winter it is that time of year,
when people prepare to spread a little Christmas cheer.
The temperature drops and the wind blows,
and on the television there are Christmas shows.
But Christmas is just one day of the year,
it is a time that people pretend to care.
But for the rest of the year they do not care,
about friends and family far or near.
So ask yourself what is Christmas to you?
and in your answer to yourself be true.

Edward Wilson

It is early in the morning as the bird's sing,
and the winter frost is covering everything.
The sky is dark with lonely streets,
as a cold wind blows taking away the heat.
Buses drive all through the night,
one an hour until the daylight.
But most people are sleeping in bed,
to the cold winter night, they are dead.
To a ringing alarm they slowly rise,
to a cold world and to cold dark skies.
Getting ready for work must be done,
in all honesty this is not fun.
Leaving the warmth of your home,
battling the cold winter morning all alone.
Getting to work to find a warm corner,
and wishing that the day will soon over.
So you can get back to where you want to be,
in your warm home resting happily.

It is getting dark and it is late in the day,
as a smelly tomcat comes out to play.
Looking through dustbins for something to eat,
if he finds a dead rat, he is in for a treat.
But his chances are thin, he will eat,
anything he finds hopefully cold meat.
Then after that he will look for some fun,
but most animals avoid him apart from one.
Flies follow him because of his smell,
truly he smell like the tomcat from hell.
It is that kind of smell that flies really digs,
but the tomcat thinks that he is truly big.
Admired by females from miles around,
but they really want to bury him in the ground.
Deep in the ground bury him and his smell,
a smell that will drive satan out of hell.
Having satan looking for a new home,
where the smell of that tomcat leaves him alone.

It is getting lighter and summer is on its way,
it means shorter nights and longer days.
That means that I can see more of you,
because you are my daydream come true.
Waking up beside you at the start of my day,
makes me love you in a very special way.
I sit on the bed and watch you sleep,
and with joy my heart softly weeps.
You are my wife and my love is very strong,
to love you any less will seem very wrong.
So I place my heart in the palm of your hands,
you are my strength and help me stand.
So you not only hold my heart but also my life,
you are everything to me and you are my wife.

It is midnight and the night is cold,
but I have my darling here to hold.
Feeling the warmth from your loving embrace,
with a loving smile on your sleepy face.
The midnight hour seems very sweet,
as your heart and my heart meet.
The clock ticks slowly the seconds away,
moving slowly towards another day.
As we fall asleep in each other's arms,
in our world of love everything is calm.
Slowly but surely the day starts to break,
later on as the alarm clock rings and we awake.
Facing the day with the memories of the night before,
those nights of passion we will have many more.

Edward Wilson

It is the time to hold you in my arms,
glazing into your eyes and feeling your charm.
Seeing your beautiful smiling face,
your love brightens up this place.
I feel your love more with each day,
I feel my love growing in every way.
I hear my heartbeat calling to you,
when I feel old, you make me feel new.
My dreams are all coming to reality,
all my dreams of you and me.
Dreams that are filling my whole life,
dreams of you and me as husband and wife.
Dreams that will never go away,
dreams that live in my heart always.
These are the dreams that I have of you,
and you are all my dreams come true.

It is the time to sleep for I am here,
in your heart, you will find me there.
As the night covers us softly,
as we sleep, you are holding me.
Dreaming of places we can go,
and seeing the love our hearts show.
Knowing that our hearts beat as one,
travelling to places in the sun.
Drifting between dream and reality,
floating together you and me.
As we sleep, we hold each other near,
so our dreams of love we can share.
Drifting away towards the light,
but sharing the magic of the night.

It is the unholy trinity three entities as one,
the spawn of Satan, his three evil sons.
The lowest of the low in all that they three do,
dragging souls of good to hell with you.
Making noise like an empty tin can,
evil children pretending to be man.
Spreading evil where ever they go,
by their fruits, them you will know.
Anti Christ and his demon friends,
they will meet a very sticky end.
The workers of the Devil on they way,
trying to spread more evil each new day.

It seems that the flies have found a new place to stay,
a place so smelly that humans stay well away.
A place where they can chew the fat,
hovering around an obnoxious tomcat.
All the flowers slowly wilt and die,
whenever that tomcat strolls by.
Producing an odour to strip paint from walls,
and birds from the sky start to fall.
He is not evil but he smell worst then hell,
the dead get up and run when they smell his smell.
A odour like no odour that came before,
worst then rotten flesh and flaming sores.
Adding insult to injury is what you will do,
if you ever let this tomcat anywhere near you.

Edward Wilson

It seems to rain on every summer weekend,
and this always drives me around the bend.
I am work hard in the sun on the weekdays,
but on the weekends the sun goes away.
In London is there a reason for this,
or is the universe trying to spread unhappiness.
The answer to this question is beyond me,
I have to accept what will be will be.
The British snow in the summer time,
has no reason and has no rhyme.
But this is a part of the British weather,
in one-day fours seasons come together.
But this happens more then twice a year,
do not take my word, you have to be there.
You have to see it to believe it,
only in Britain does this weather fit.
I was born in London but I still can not see,
why the summer wants to rain on me.

It was a dark night in the city,
the wind blows showing no pity.
The shadows move down lonely streets,
The wind takes away any heat.
The trees cast shadows in the moonlight,
as the wind blows throughout the night.
The rain of the night is sweeping,
through all this the moon is shining.
Casting moonbeams to the ground,
as the rain is falling all around.
Night clouds are moving by,
as the rain falls from the sky.
Lightning strikes lighting up the night,
as the thunder rolls behind the light.
The wind starts to get stronger,
blowing branches into one another.
The storm is preparing to rage on,
but as the daybreaks it fades and is gone.
The world wakes to a wet day,
as slowly the sun dries the rain away.

King Louie has got married; he has taken a wife,
and I hope that he is happy for the rest of his life.
But meanwhile there is big trouble in paradise,
as the son of Satan is rolling the dice.
Rebelling and leading others astray,
being loud with his insults everyday.
Trying to bring others to their knees,
and spreading discord as he please.
He has his minions, those that follow,
listening to his empty word that are hollow.
As he jumps up and down shouting,
his words are nothing but wind.
But there are those that do not know,
but every so often his evil will show.
Through the mask that he wears,
only for himself, does he really care.

King Louie swings through the racking silently,
as King Kong's secret son roaming free.
Spying on the humans down below,
looking for mistakes everywhere he goes.
He is supposed to be health and safety,
but in times of trouble he simply flees.
To find some nuts to eat, please understand,
he is a racking dwelling primate, an orang-utan.
When health and safety issues come up he will hide,
he will find a cardboard box and climb inside.
He will wait until the threat has gone,
and come out of hiding and carry on.
Swinging silently through the racking,
looking for nuts that he can be eating.

Edward Wilson

Last night I fell asleep thinking about you,
and I dreamed that you would always be true.
The darkness of the night covered me,
from my dreams your face I can see.
Slowly I drift away in your arms,
I feel relaxed and I feel calm.
The fear off the night I no longer feel,
because my dreams of you are real.
The seconds seem like days to me,
my dreams seem like my reality.
I feel no fear with you by my side,
holding my hand and being my guide.
Drifting into a world of uncertainty,
but I am happy because you are with me.
But then the alarm bell rings to wake me,
and I hear you sleeping beside me.
So you own my dreams and also my heart,
and you live in them both even if we are apart.

Let the morning find us as the night left us here,
in each other's arms and holding each other near.
Let the dreams that we shared last night,
stay with us well into the daylight.
Let our two hearts beating as one,
remembering all the things we done.
Looking at you in the morning as you sleep,
wondering of the secrets that you keep.
Feeling your body next to mine,
tied together by an invisible line.
To the magic moments that we share,
opening my heart so you can live there.

Lights are flashing in my head,
am I still alive or am I dead.
This feeling is really bothering me,
all these flashing lights that I see.
It feels like my head is caving in,
and now all the pains begin.
My arms ache and also my feet,
my heart seems to be missing beats.
I can not focus because I can not see,
someone tell me what is happening to me.
I sit in silence listening to voices in my head,
I do not understand a word that is said.
But I still try to hang onto life,
with all it's trouble and strife.
While there is life there is hope,
do not give up your life and be a dope.

Lights in the shy that shine down on me,
shining lights that help me to see.
Lights that are burning very bright,
lights that shine through the night.
Lights in the heavens everyday,
some so dim, but they never fade away
Lights that shine in the morning light,
are the same lights that shine at night.
The lights we see but do not care,
lights in the sky that are always there.
Lights of warmth on a cold day,
and lights that helps me on my way.

Lights in the sky in the middle of the night,
as they move towards the daylight.
Carrying lovers from far and wide,
back to their waiting lover's side.
The roar of the engines as the aeroplane comes to land,
as standing at these moments has now been banded.
The comes to a stop and people leave,
back on solid ground you are relieved.
Walking through customs on your way out,
hundreds of people are walking about.
Custom officers are waiting to grab you,
because they have nothing else better to do.
turning your bags inside out,
all you want to do is to get out.
As they leave, you must pack your bags again,
Custom officers drive me round the bend.
Leaving the airport with someone that loves you,
as you leave behind those aeroplane blues.

Looking for an answer to how this can be,
why a circus let it's orang-utan go free.
How that orang-utan could work as health and safety,
a tree dwelling primate that is looking out for me.
Something else I can not understand,
is why this orang-utan thinks he is a man?
I do not know who you think you are,
or how managed to buy yourself a car.
You seem to have turned your back on your past,
and you seem to be living your life very fast.
You are swinging through the trees no more,
or scrapping your knuckles along the floor.
You are the son of King Kong; you can not escape that,
even if you have traded your crown for a hard hat.

Looking for love in the fields of gold,
sheep are easy, or so you are told.
Because of your body odour humans avoid you,
so the next link in the chain are sheep for you.
Forget about wellington boots, they are no good,
get next to a sheep and surprise it if you could.
Maybe while the sheep is eating some grass,
your smell will hit her first so you better move fast.
Unless you paralyse the sheep with your breath,
all the others will leave so there is only one left.
But your body odour will bring it back to life,
and it will run like you were the farmer with a knife.
So Mr tomcat you will have to go back home,
to sleeping in your cardboard box all alone.

Looking into the morning at the rising of the sun,
thinking about yesterday and all that we done.
Looking forward to the fun of today,
trying everything to make you want to stay.
Feeling the magic that comes from your touch,
my darling I truly do love you very much.
I plan to shower you with all that I can give,
not just in my arms but my heart also to live.
As I thing all this while listening to you sleep,
knowing that my love for you is very deep.
So I close my eyes and put my arms around you,
and I sleep knowing that my love for you is true.

Edward Wilson

Looking through my window into the morning light,
noticing that the world has turned white.
All night long silently snow fell from the sky,
as the winter clouds are slowly blown by.
As the temperature drops and the morning is cold,
I wish I had you in my loving arms to hold.
I know that one-day you will be mine,
but I find it hard to wait until that time.
I want to give you all my heart,
which aches whenever we are apart.
But I must be brave and I must be strong,
for the sake of my heart I will carry on.
Through the snow and through the rain,
so I can be in your presence once again.

My darling wife is gently sleeping beside me,
listening to my darling wife breathe softly.
Thinking about her loveliness as she sleeps,
having her love in my heart to keep.
Feeling every movement that she makes,
and with every touch, my breath she takes.
Living everyday one moment at a time,
loving her every moment is blowing my mind.
Looking to the early morning sun,
knowing that she is my only one.
She is my angel for the rest of my life,
always and forever my darling wife.

Not just a dream but also a fantasy,
this and more is what you are to me.
When you are near my heart skips a beat,
and I shake from my head to my feet.
You are not aware of what you do to me,
you make my trapped heart run free.
Moving toward you one step at a time,
I feel confused but I am also fine.
I do not understand these feeling in my heart,
that keep me awake when we are apart.
These feelings that grow more and more,
that have doubled in size from the day before.
Bigger then me and bigger then you,
a beating heart that is strong and true.
Holding the essence of my love,
that will fit you like a velvet glove.
Protecting you and keeping you warm,
as together we weather life's storm.

One man and his dog are playing out and away,
trying to find a new reason to be happy everyday.
On a winter's day, he ties his dog to a fence,
or in the park, he will tie her to a park bench.
Then go to see another dog miles away,
and stay there for a couple of days.
Straying from home to find another,
is this other dog just a friend or a lover?
The man will never let his dog know,
when he abandons her, where he goes.
Despite this treatment that the dog gets,
with the memory span of a goldfish, she forgets.
But while he leaves his dog, she is playing too,
and from other dogs getting some special brew.
The brew is strong, but not strong enough,
lacking the power to put her up the duff.
This is something that superman can not do,
but superman will never want to get next to you.

Edward Wilson

Over the hills and running far away,
towards the dawn of a brand new day.
Leaving the sorrow far behind,
and new happiness hoping to find.
Running away from the sunset,
running from a day you want to forget.
Running fast into the dark night,
running towards the daylight.
Running through the night passing the moon,
and you know that it will be daylight soon.
In the sunlight leave your troubles behind,
and in the morning happiness you may find.

Reaching for you the love of my life,
holding you near my darling wife.
Looking into your eyes in the morning light,
or holding you in the middle of the night.
These are the things that I hold dear,
and in my heart you are there.
The years rush by, but I still love you,
you are my life and my dream come true.
Even that noise you make as you sleep,
lets me know that you sleep is deep.
But it also lets me understand,
throughout my life you will hold my hand.
Walking with me side by side,
with a proud love we will never hide.

Secret lovers loving in the past,
hiding feelings that may never last.
Dreaming of moments between us two,
moments shared between me and you.
That tender moment of love's soft touch,
moments of magic that prove too much.
Stealing looks in a crowded room,
hoping that we can be together soon.
Fighting these feeling we have for each other,
knowing that we belong to another.
So we keep our secrets locked in our hearts,
so we are together even when we are apart.

Sitting in the park under an oak tree,
the sun is shining and children run free.
Children on bikes riding around,
as the wind lifts litter from the ground.
A lady walking her dog in the park,
there is a party that will carry on into the dark.
A DJ playing some good soul music,
people dancing, this is a big hit.
A lady cooking chicken for sale,
A smell so good it can not fail.
looking at people as they paint their face,
enjoying the day in a wonderful place.
The wind is blowing a little strong,
but the party in the park carries on.
People everywhere doing what they want to do,
to themselves they are being true.
Reliving their childhood once again,
meeting and making old and new friends.

Edward Wilson

Sleep my little one and do not fear the night,
I am here to watch over you until the daylight.
I will share with you all that is in my head,
I will hold you softly as you sleep in bed.
I will watch over you as you dream at night,
in your dream world that is far from my sight.
The noise that you make as you sleep,
is because your breathing is very deep.
I am here for you through rain or shine,
and I hold your love in this heart of mine.
You are my future and you are my life,
you are my little piggy and you are my wife.

Sleeping on a settee in the middle of the sitting room,
as the flies gather around me, I must get up soon.
Wipe my face with a muddy and soiled leaf,
then with a toilet brush, brush my teeth.
Then take my clothes of to get some air,
until they smell fresh, now them I can wear.
Off to work after I have eaten my breakfast,
I just hope that my body odour will last.
I feed the cockroaches that are my pets,
and my hair lice that I should not forget.
Now with my toilet brush I brush my hair,
now I am ready to go anywhere.
I get on the bus and then after I slowly walk,
nobody wants to know me, so to myself I talk.
Telling myself I smell so super sweet,
from my lice filled hair to my mouldy feet.
It is a fashion statement that I make,
as a tomcat, a bath I will never take.

Soap and water in a bath or a kitchen sink,
wash daily or you may begin to stink.
Brush or comb your hair once a day,
washing your hair may keep lice away.
Brush your teeth and keep them clean,
or they may begin to turn a shade of green.
Dried on sweat and dirty cloths is not a turn on,
members of the opposite sex will be gone.
Body odours are hidden with water and soap,
without them you really stand no hope.
Of getting a partner someone to keep,
so you may be better off with a sheep.
Because no human being will stay with you,
because washing is something you will not do.

Soap and water, washing your skin,
is part of how basic hygiene begins.
Taking a toothbrush and using it,
for your mouth, it is designed to fit.
But you use it as a toilet brush,
it seems your brain has turned to mush.
You take a bath about once a year,
while your body odour follow you everywhere.
The lifestyle you are living seems to please you,
and washing is a concept that you do not do.
That is why you live on a settee alone,
because no one wants to take you home.
It is not just you, but that odour too,
because that odour always follows you.

Edward Wilson

Some days have sunshine and some days have rain,
some days I am calm and some days I feel insane.
Some days there is wind and clouds in my sky,
on days like these I barely make it by.
Bu there are also days of sunshine,
where my peaceful state on mind I find.
A balance between these days is hard to see,
because the balance resides within me.
If my emotions are off then it may rain,
and I will have a nasty headache again.
But if my emotions are steady and I am fine,
then my day will be filled with sunshine.

Stolen glances each time you are near,
you are my darling and this is clear.
Your tender touch as your hand meets mine,
your loving smile so soft and kind.
The words that you speak so softly,
have a soothing effect on me.
Your hair so gently as it falls,
to you my love I give my all.
The day seems long until I see you,
holding you near is what I want to do.
But you belong to someone else,
so my feeling of love stay on the shelf.
In my heart each night I cry,
man be strong at least try.

Summer is over and winter is truly hear,
as that cold crisp feeling fills the air.
The wind is blowing a little cold,
as the leaves from the trees it holds.
The flowers have gone away to sleep,
as the temperature drop very steep.
The sky turns grey as the rain starts to fall,
raining on everyone great and small.
The swans are flying to places new,
every year this is what they do.
Humans also like to get far away,
to somewhere where they are warmer days.
With warmer nights and love in the air,
and warm feelings of love to share.

Summer nights that were here,
too much heat for me to care.
The winter season is here at last,
unfortunately it moves too fast.
The winter brings rain and snow,
and grey clouds in the sky show.
The wind blows throughout the day,
blowing the rain clouds away.
The leaves that are leaving the trees,
blown away by the winter breeze.
As the darkness falls, the night gets cold,
keep yourself warm and do not be bold.
Do not go out unless you have too,
keeping warm is what you must do.
The days get shorter in the winter light,
still twenty-four hours but longer nights.

Edward Wilson

Sweating toxic odours while I sleep on my settee,
what I ate yesterday is sweating out of me.
I am wearing the same clothes that I wore the night before,
so the toxic odours seem to be increasing even more.
Filling the room with a radio active gas,
it is without any form and without any mass.
But I am also breathing in a deep sleep,
outside the room all the flies keep.
But some will venture in and drop dead,
as I sleep on my settee that doubles as a bed.
Cockroaches gasping and crying for breathe,
very soon only their shell will be left.
As they dissolve quickly in the toxic fume,
that is now filling up my bedroom.
Killing inserts and flies both left and right,
they will be my breakfast at the end of the night.
After breakfast I will get on the morning bus,
taking my time to work because there is no rush.
Breathing on paint and watching it bubble,
ordinarily I would get into big trouble.
But with a breathe that can melt steel,
no body thinks that I am for real.
There is more to me and that is the truth,
not just a tomcat, do you want proof?

Swinging through the trees is near to my heart,
but swinging through the racking is a world apart.
Climbing trees meant everything to me,
climbing the shelving is different you see.
Hanging out with the other orang-utans,
but now I chill out with the humans.
I try to fit in so I shave my face,
to an orang-utan this is a disgrace.
King Kong my father told me,
to be the best orang-utan that I can be.
So I will try to fit in the best that I can,
the son of King Kong an orang-utan.

Swinging through the trees on my way to work,
I am just an orang-utan and not a big jerk.
Imitating humans is what I love to do,
if you are in authority I will imitate you.
I sit behind the wheel a car trying to steer,
as I make sure that the coast is clear.
Then I drive my car down the street,
as an orang-utan I have fingers on my feet.
So pushing the pedals is something new to me,
but I will get the hang of it, just wait and see.
The son of a king, but doing health and safety,
I shaved my face so they do not know it is me.
I hang out in the racking like it is a playpen,
swinging through the racking again and again.
This is like the jungle, a home from home,
with no other orang-utans here I am alone.
But that means there is more food for me,
as the son of King Kong I live happily.

Swinging through the trees with the breeze in my hair,
this is a feeling that my new human wife can share.
Eating bananas and walking on all fours,
to her sheltered life I have opened up new doors.
Now she can see through my eyes,
now she knows I never told her lies.
Taking shelter in the trees at night,
sleeping under the bright moonlight.
To rest from the animals down below,
nasty animals with big teeth to show.
Dangerous animals like the maga-rats,
also savage animals like the big cats.
I dream of Luke Skywalker and I use the force,
I am not a Jedi but an orang-utan off course.
Hiding away from other baboons,
hoping to be in civilisation soon.
As King Louie this is my domain,
because I am the only one with a brain.

Edward Wilson

Take me in the morning and hold me tight,
hold me like you held me all last night.
Listen to my heart beating at your touch,
the happiness and joy are all too much.
My head spins and my mouth is dry,
I can not control myself, but I try.
I have found love and joy in your arms,
you have taken my will with your charm.
The light through the window softly shines,
as our sweat covered body intertwine.
I look into your eyes as you sleep,
not knowing the secrets that you keep.
But the secrets that I keep in my heart,
wishing that you and I would never part.

The actions of a snake in the grass is not plain to see,
but he slivers around people like you and me.
Smiling in your face and stabbing you in the back,
this is how a snake in the grass will attack.
Not really a human being, but all snake,
wherever he goes trouble he will make.
Sliding in and out of corners and places,
hurting all the people from different races.
He does not care if you are black or white,
just as long as he can drag you out of sight.
With people to hurt as he walks through life,
his slippery tongue is as sharp as a knife.
Spreading confusion and unhappiness,
he is only happy when he is doing this.
A rat in the clothing of a rattle snake,
A vampire looking for blood to take.
A great white shark dressed up as a dog,
a cobra waiting under a log.
These are the things that he will do,
waiting quietly so he can destroy you.

The clock has gone forward by an hour,
so I get up one hour earlier and have a shower.
then get ready and what I must do,
leaving for work, but also leaving you.
As you lay in bed are you aware?
that I slipped away and I am not there.
To hold you gently as you sweetly sleep,
and all your dreams that you keep.
I take my keys and get into my car,
and drive fifteen minutes from where you are.
We are over seven thousands heartbeats apart,
but you still live here in my beating heart.
Unaware of my counting heart,
that knows how long we are apart.
But I know that I will come home to you,
because you my wife and my dream come true.

The day is dawning but the moon is still high,
casting shadows as thin clouds float by.
No longer navy but a lighter blue,
at this time sleeping is what people do.
So people miss the beauty of the sinking moon,
as the sun rises there will be daylight soon.
The birds are still in their nests fast asleep,
safe from human eyes they try to keep.
As the sun rises at the start of the day,
gently pushing the darkness away.
Turning the sky a flaming red,
it is worth you getting out of bed.
To see nature in all it's finest,
only for an hour then it is finish.
Then the sky tuns a sea blue,
as the sun shines down on you.

Edward Wilson

The feeling of winter is in the air,
as frost and snow is everywhere.
The day is cold as the frost sets in,
and out of the sky it is snowing.
There is a strong winter breeze,
and there are snow-covered trees.
The day wears on and turns to night,
as the snow reflects the moonlight.
The land is covered in deep snow,
as a strong winter breeze blows.
The clouds are moving across the sky,
and sweeping snow goes sweeping by.
Steam rises from houses on the street,
as people surround themselves with heat.
The central heating is running high,
to keep warm the people try.
Covering themselves in warm blankets,
covering their body; every little bit.
As the temperature sink low,
in strong winds and blinding snow.
The night turns into a blizzard,
with many dangers and hazards.
As the children in bed are warm,
sleeping deeply unaware of the storm.

The feelings that I have when you are near,
they seem strange and are not very clear.
The love that I feel in my heart for you,
makes me confused when I am around you.
The dreams that I have in my heart,
keeps me warm when we are apart.
Your arms, your legs your head and your face,
your coat, your jacket and your dress of lace.
The breath that you breathe is soft and sweet,
your style and grace knocks me of my feet.
Time waits for no one but I will wait a lifetime for you,
you are my fantasy and all my dreams come true.

The frost covers the whole land,
the middle of winter is now at hand.
The temperature drops very low,
the people may expect some snow.
The sun has not yet shown its head,
and most of the world is warm in bed.
As the wind blows through the streets,
robbing the place of all its heat.
As the snow slowly starts to fall,
on every car, tree, house and wall.
As the world turns and the sun will shine,
the temperature will rise and the day seems fine.
When you compare it to the night before,
that made you want to go inside and lock the door.

The heat of the morning and the cold of the night,
the feeling that I get from having you in my sight.
The love that I have in my heart for you,
with each heartbeat my heart calls you.
I think of your long flowing hair,
and I wish that I had you here.
The way that you move as you walk,
your soft and tender words as you talk.
Your soft skin as it touches mine,
my darling you really blow my mind.
I feel happy whenever you are around,
as strange as all this may really sound.
This is the meaning of my love for you,
and to my heart I will always be true.

Edward Wilson

The land is dark and the land is getting cold,
the winter season has taken a firm hold.
The rain is falling as drops of ice,
this freezing weather is not very nice.
The birds of the morning no longer sing,
in the early hours of the freezing morning.
As the day goes by the temperature will rise,
when the sun may appear in the winter sky.
But it is still cold enough for snow to fall,
enough snow to make snowmen and snowballs.
The lake has frozen over like a stone,
this weather will chill you to the bone.
A cold and bitter wind blows,
blowing the rain and the snow.
Blowing the snow into doorways,
this is just the start of the day.
As the sun rises and the wind blows,
reflecting sunlight on the winter snow.

The light from the window is coming through,
as you lay in bed, the light is shining on you.
As you lay there sleeping gently,
I know that you mean the world to me.
Our bedroom is filled by the morning light,
at the end of a wonderfully peaceful night.
Waking from the dreams of the night,
slowly looking into the morning light.
Not quiet asleep and not quiet awake,
it is the time for decisions to make.
Get ready for work or staying in bed,
these are the things in my head.
Drive to work or stay right here,
what I want to do is simple and clear.
But I go to work to pay the bills,
of manual labour I have had my fill.
I want to escape to the sun with my wife,
and live there happily for the rest of my life.

The light of the morning fades from night to day,
as the world spins moving the night away.
The wind is still and there is no sound,
no leaves being blown to the ground.
There is a silence over the land,
there is no movement from beast or man.
Suddenly lightning fills the shy,
as storm clouds slowly roll by.
Lightning strikes and thunder crashes,
as these elements start to clash.
The wind joins in, as does the rain,
as the four elements fight again.
No element loses and no element wins,
not the wind, rains, thunder or lightning.
But they continue to fight putting on a show,
as quickly as they came is how they will go.

The light of the morning fills the sky,
orange clouds of the sunrise float by.
The wind of the morning softly blows,
passed the trees on the street it slowly goes.
The willow weeps at the start of the day,
as the rising sun gets on it way.
Rising slowly into the morning sky,
as a flock of geese go flying by.
The grass by the roadside sways in the wind,
is this a summer or a winter morning?
Will there be sunshine or will there be snow?
here in London no one really knows.
Is it winter, autumn, summer or spring?
or is it just another London morning.

Edward Wilson

The lights are dim but not as dim as you,
are you aware of the job that you do?
Are you even aware of what you should be?
according to you, you are health and safety.
But you swing through the racking looking at men,
your desire to be human is driving you around the bend.
You think that your employers think you are a man,
to tell the truth you really are an orang-utan.
You are Pinocchio of the jungle and animal world,
in an attempt to be human, you grab a human girl.
She knows you are an orang-utan but she only believes,
that you are just a human that eats lot of leaves.
Sometimes in amazement she stands to look,
as you act out parts from the jungle book.
Your employers knows you are an orang-utan but,
they keep quiet so they can pay you peanuts.

The lights in the morning that no one really sees,
the gently smells carried on the morning breeze.
The morning sun rising into the morning sky,
as the morning birds go flying slowly by.
The world is spinning round and round,
always spinning but making no sound.
In London four season happen in one day,
it is the season of discontent, as they will say.
But I live happily where I call home,
as long as people leave me alone.
For the place I live is beautiful too,
with endless things that I can do.

The lights in the morning that shine through my window,
is a very beautiful and awesome early morning show.
The wind that blows in the morning light,
is the same wind that blows through the night.
The clouds that move in from the night,
are the clouds that share the daylight.
The singing birds that live in the trees,
singing through the morning breeze.
Inserts crawling looking for food,
looking for something good.
The lights of the morning slowly change,
in the daylight hours they re arrange.
Into the your day come rain or shine,
it may be cloudy or it may be fine.
So enjoy your day if you can,
and do not bury your head in the sand.

The love I had for you has now gone away,
now I have l to face a new empty day
A day without your love in my life,
a day where I am balancing on a knife.
A day where all my worries are here,
a day where you are no longer near.
A day full of sorrow and full of pain,
a day of no sunshine but only rain.
A day where I cook for myself,
and I try to put my feelings on the shelf.
But my feelings will not let me forget you,
so I know just what I have to do.
I have to find you and make things right,
The problems must be solved this night.
So we can be together once again,
not just lovers but also best friends.

Edward Wilson

The love that I feel in the daylight,
is the same love that I feel late at night.
The things I see as I look into your eyes,
they humble me and cut me down to size.
I am a child in your loving embrace,
with the glow of love shining in your face.
You are the one that I wake up next to,
and all my heart I give to you.
I know that I love you in my heart,
from now to forever we will never part.
You are my dream and my fantasy,
and you mean the world to me.
So hold my hand, as we grow old together,
because I know that I will leave you never.

The moonlight in the morning shines until day breaks,
and then the light of the sun will slowly overtake.
To hide the moonlight with the ray of the sunlight,
the sunshine for the day and the moonlight for the night.
As the world spins and night turns to day,
to their part of the day different animals stay.
Humans mostly work in the daylight,
but foxes mostly hunt in the night.
In the daytime foxes mostly sleep,
to this pattern the foxes try to keep.
Throughout all this the world goes around,
slowly spinning without making a sound.

The morning is very cold as the sun starts to rise,
as the temperature tries to reach it highs.
Slowly climbing one step at a time,
not knowing if the day will be fine.
The wind is blowing down the street,
taking away that rising heat.
The clouds are gathering fast,
will it rain and will it last?
The heat of the morning being carried away,
is a sign that it will be a cold wet day.
This is just the start of another summer's day,
in London where winter weather always stay.

The morning light shines on your face,
as the day is dawning here in this place.
I roll over and hold you in my arms,
as you sleep I will keep you from harm.
Physical harm will not come near you,
and our lives the Lord God I give too.
I want to keep you safe, but I am only a man,
but the future belongs to God, can you understand.
So this I pray every night and everyday,
the love I have for my wife will never fade away.
As the years pass by and we grow old,
in each other's arms to have and to hold.

Edward Wilson

The morning moon is high the sky,
a tropical breeze blow the clouds by.
So that the sky is cold and clear,
as the wind is blowing everywhere.
The branches are bending in the wind,
as the grass seems to be bowing.
As the sun appears in the jealous sky,
and orange clouds go rushing by.
The sun rises as the moon looks on,
as the tropical breeze is blowing strong.
The wind is blowing the leaves form the trees,
being blown about in this tropical breeze.

The morning sun and the clock on the wall,
The leaves to the ground they gently fall.
The wind that blows and the grass that sways,
all this is happening at the start of the day.
The rain that falls softly from the sky,
a flock of birds that are flying by.
The water running down the drain,
it is all part of the gentle rain.
The clouds that are drifting low,
creating fog as they slowly go.
The sun in the sky rises slowly,
for all the people of the world to see.
The earth in space slowly spins,
so the night ends and the day begins.

The New Year has started and promises were made,
but after a day or so the promises start to fade.
The plans that you made for the coming year,
made at a moment's notice and are no longer there.
The determination left with the song and the wine,
and in the sober light of day it seems to be fine.
The promises that you had made for the coming year,
now seem small and furthermore you do not care.
So in your weaken state you will carrying on,
in a re-cycling circle until the year has gone.
The same group of people that you see once a year,
belittling you because they really do not care.
But you are there because you want to progress,
but behind the senses their life is a mess.
But you are unaware of the path they walk,
and you are unaware of their lies as they talk.
But for the rest of the year you feel fine,
but you get closer to crossing that line.
The point of no return on the other side,
where all your darkness you must hide.

The night is cold and the winter is here,
as the winter frost is gathering everywhere.
The streets are empty and very cold.
and the winter wind is getting bold.
As the wind blows alone the streets,
adding to the cold winter heat.
The trees look scary and very bare,
as the leaves are being blown everywhere.
Snow falling gently to the ground,
on the howling wind blown all around.
The sun is not rising into the sky,
as the night clouds go flying by.
The night goes on until the day is dawning,
and the sun will rise on this winter's morning.

The night is coming and the land is cold,
you may need someone in your life to hold.
A strong winter wind moves through the street,
there is only emptiness the wind will meet.
People are wrapped up warm safe in bed,
visions of warmer days in their head.
But the wind still blows and snow is falling,
as the world now is silently sleeping.
The birds have now left town,
because the winter has come around.
Through the winter some animals sleep,
out of sight all winter they keep.
Waking up as the month get warm,
when there are no more winter storms.
No more blizzards and no more snow,
and the new leaves start to show.

The night is coming and the land is dark,
as he takes his dog for a walk in the park.
His dog sold her kennel for a kennel for two,
but his dog was told this is not the right thing to do.
Because her master has another dog near by,
and too sneak away to be with her he will try.
Using the excuse that he is going to fish,
thinking his second dog is a better dish.
So he will leave his first dog in the kennel for two,
and when he get there, he will know what to do.
He loves dog number two more then dog number one,
because dog number one is just for having some fun.
Like chasing buses and fetching a stick,
but in all other areas she makes him sick.
Dog number two is also for having fun,
but with more history, there is more they have done.
While he is asleep, his dog will curl up at his back,
but these feeling for dog number one he lacks.
Dog number two wakes him up with a kiss,
but dog number one he never will miss.
The error has been done; the mistake has been made,
for the kennel for two dog number one already paid.

The night is long and the streets are cold,
we all need someone special to hold.
The daylight hours seem to be less,
winter is in full swing I must confess.
The leaves have fallen from the trees,
carried away by the cold winter breeze.
The clouds of the skies are sinking low,
creating fog but not rain or snow.
The temperature is dropping rapidly,
with frozen patches for all to see.
The rain falls and the snow flies,
falling slowly from winter skies.
Coming to rest on the frozen ground,
forming a blanket of white all around.

The night is not yet over but the day has begun,
I lay here waiting for the rising of the sun.
The moon that is in charge of the night,
seems to shy away from the daylight.
The shadows of the night exist also in the day,
reaching inward and out but not fading away.
The stars in the night sky not visible in the day,
The night wind that blows in the daylight,
and the temperature drops during the night.
The light of the sun heats the day,
but as the sun sets the heat fades away.
Leaving the chill of the cold night,
staying away from the heat of daylight.

Edward Wilson

The night is surrounding us as the land gets dark,
the night has dealt its hand and left its mark.
The shadows are gathering around you and me,
the darkness of the night is all we can see.
The struggle of the endless night is ahead of us,
in the storms of the darkness in the light we trust.
Holding on to each other and never letting go,
how long is this night, I really do not know.
But we have each other through thick and thin,
and by your side I will always be standing.
With a glimmer of hope at the first light of day,
as the long night starts to slowly fades away.
The world is full of hope after the long night,
and the love of GOD guides us in the light.

The night time hours are full of a nasty aroma,
a most horrible and truly distasteful body odour.
A smell like blocked drains on steroids to the power of X,
I would truly hate to think about what will come next.
Breathe that smells like fertiliser from a cow's behind,
do not breath in this direction, if you don't mind.
The fire in your hands are toxic to the touch,
with an overwhelming after-shave that is too much.
Essence of tomcat is your own brand,
hoping a big contract you it will land.
It will never in a million years be a Christmas socking filler,
it is more likely to be used as a heavy duty fly killer.
It is your own design and be proud of that,
so go out and buy some Essence of tomcat.

The rain is falling outside my window,
it may fall all day, I really do not know.
The daylight is here but the sun hides its face,
the outside world seems like a cold grey place.
I sit in my bed thinking about what to do,
or should I lay down and sleep next to you.
I feel hungry and so I will get something to eat,
I think that I want to eat something very sweet.
But there is nothing sweet in my home,
so I sit in bed listening to my tummy moan.
I look at my wife as she softly sleeps,
listening to her breathing slow and deep.
Her little face resting so peacefully,
wishing that you are dreaming of me.
I hope that you are but I am not sure,
so I will let you sleep a little more.
So sleep my darling for I am here,
and to your heart I am always near.

The snow of the night falls on the high ground,
slowly spreading to the cities that are all around.
The wind is blowing the falling snow far,
shortly it may reach where you are.
The sky is grey with snow clouds of white,
as the sunshine filters through as grey light.
The snow falls slowly as it falls all day,
a soft# wind to blow the clouds away.
Footprints appear in the fresh snow,
as of to work people carefully go.
Children rush outside ready to play,
so much snow so there is no school today.
Making balls and men of snow,
the children are happy and it shows.
Children are dancing in the street,
playing in the snow with happy feet.

Edward Wilson

The stars in the sky giving us light,
shining by day and shining by night.
Filling the sky with their glow,
but in the daylight they do not show.
So is the love that I have for you,
a love that is pure, a love that is true.
A love that is not always clear,
but a love that is always there.
A love that watches over you,
that will protect you in all you do.
Keeping you safe day by day,
a love that will never go away.
This the love that I have in my heart,
a love that will never fall apart.

The strong winter wind blows down the street,
moving fast and chasing away any kind of heat.
The moon is high in the winter sky,
and the winter nights move slowly by.
It is in the darkness that the rat does his thing,
trying his hardest to mess up everything.
He is a rat in the clothes of a snake,
everything he says is a lie; he is a fake.
Moving through the day with his ponytail,
spreading lies and then he will bail.
Out the back door were he got in,
wherever he is trouble will begin.
His odour is off coffee and smoke,
his odour is strong this is no joke.
But from his high chair he looks down,
causing trouble for all those around.
One day he will fall of his high chair,
and when that happens I want to be there.

The wind blows through the listening trees,
as the trees start talking in the breeze.
The wind moves through the lowly grass,
and down the roads the wind will pass.
Into the houses and down the lane,
blowing in the sunshine and in the rain.
In the morning the win will blow,
when will it stop or where does it go.
The wind blows through rain or shine,
if the day is dark or the day is fine.
The wind blows into the night,
and is still blowing at daylight.
The blowing wind can make your day,
blowing all the storm clouds away.
But the clouds are filters of the sunlight,
so the day does not seem too bright.

The wind in my face and snow on the mountain top,
I hope that the falling snow will never stop.
The cold crisp wind blowing in my face,
the winter wind blowing through this place.
People skiing and having a good time,
in the cold clear air I am feeling fine.
I can not ski, so I just sit and look,
and maybe I would try to read a book.
But with all this beauty around me,
watching nature at it purest, naturally.
As the sunlight reflects of the snow,
from this place I never want to go.
Here with nature feeling at one,
also enjoying the winter sun.

Edward Wilson

The wind in the trees strong as it blows,
the winter rain gives way to snow.
The leaves have left the trees bear,
with the signs of winter everywhere.
The winter clouds in a winter sky,
with the winter wind blowing by.
The cold air is surrounding this place,
it comes and it goes without a trace.
But its presence can be felt as it goes,
and the effects of the wind shows.
This is just another winter morning,
just before the day is dawning.
The winter wind blows the night clouds away,
as the world turns to reveal another winter's day.

The wind is blowing and snow is falling in the street,
while in his box a tomcat can smell his feet.
The low clouds are turning the night white,
as the tomcat is hiding out of sight.
Looking for some food blowing by,
then out of his box he will fly.
Sharing his home with a big rat,
living together a rat and a tomcat.
Sharing a moment of tenderness,
living together in true happiness.
While the wind blows up a storm,
the tomcat and the rat keep each other warm.
When the storm is over will they still be friends?
or will the rat come to a very sticky end?
The snow is melting and runs downs the drains,
while with hunger the tomcat goes insane.
Jumping at the rat, the tomcat wants to eat,
but the rat is very quick on his feet.
Running fast down the drain,
never to smell the tomcat again.

The wind is blowing as the rain falls down,
falling hard and soaking the ground.
The clouds are gathering in the wind,
it looks like a storm is about to begin.
As the rain gathers forming lakes,
the drains are blocked so the water waits.
The cars drive through as the water sprays,
forcing the water out of the way.
The sky slowly starts to turn grey,
with thunderclouds rolling this way.
The sky lights up as lightning flashes,
with distance rumbles as thunder crashes.
The clouds are full with rain,
that can not flow down the drain.
So the rain gathers with nowhere to go,
it will dry up but it will be very slow.

The wind is blowing hard outside my window,
why it is blowing so hard I really do not know.
It is a summer's morning so it should be warm,
but instead the wind is blowing up a storm.
The trees are being blown to and fro,
and the leaves of the trees just let go.
Blowing away from the trees,
caught up in this very strong breeze.
The night clouds are making way,
for the morning blue sky of the day.
The grass of the ground is swaying,
in this strong wind that is blowing.
The birds are hiding in the trees,
keeping out of the strong breeze.

Edward Wilson

It The wind is blowing on a cold winter's day;
the leaves from trees are being blown away.
The temperature is changing in the wind,
the wind is harsh and very unkind.
Blowing the people and forcing them back,
showing no mercy and showing no tact.
The rain starts to fall gently at first,
then without warning that is a huge burst.
As the wind picks up harder then before,
blowing more leaves to the floor.
The rain is being blown across the street,
in the skies the thunder and the lightning meet.
Lighting up the skies with lightning flashes,
listening to the thunder as it crashes.
It may be day but the sky is grey,
as the light seems to fade away.
Into the darkness of the night,
under the pale moonlight.

The wind is blowing through your hair,
and the summer nights are no longer here.
As the autumn season is winding down,
and autumn leaves are falling to the ground.
I stand here looking into your eyes,
by your beauty I am hypnotised.
The magic that lives in your smile,
together with your gentle style.
It makes me want to drift away,
so we can be together always.
As I brush your hair from your face,
as long as we are together I love this place.
I reach out and gently pull you near,
as my face is touched by your hair.
I wish this moment will never end,
because you are more then a friend.

The wind is moving through the trees,
in the form of a winter's breeze.
There is also an orang-utan swinging by,
with his big plans he aims for the sky.
First he wanted to learn to create fire,
but being human is his true desire.
Copying human each and everyday,
listening and copying what they say.
Buying a car so he blends in,
and within himself he has a grin.
Thinking that he has got away with it,
but you are fooling no one, a bit.
So chase your dreams and every desire,
but you will never be able to make fire.

The wind of the morning blows through the sky,
as the world spins blowing the night clouds by.
The sky is changing colour as this takes place,
slowly as the sun rises the night starts to race.
Away from the morning and away from the light,
back into the darkness, back into the night.
As the sun rises it brings warm air,
is the day going to be cold or fair?
The temperature is higher then the night,
as the sunrises bringing the morning light.
The birds wake and start to sing,
they do this every morning.
Weather it is sunshine or raining,
you will hear the birds singing.

Edward Wilson

The wind of the morning moves through the trees,
shaking the branches in a cold winter's breeze.
The streets are empty and the roads are cold,
to venture into the streets show that you are bold.
But school is calling me to be there,
going to school in the winter is not fair.
Battling through the snow and ice,
in winter conditions that are not very nice.
But getting to school seeing all my friends,
makes me happy because I can play again.
The school is warm as I play all day,
but as school is closing, I have to go away.
Going back home to where I can be warm,
to keep me safe from the winter storms.

The wind of the morning talks to the trees,
as it takes the leaves and blow them free.
The moonlight shines on the world below,
as the moonlight shadows begin to show.
The temperature drops because there is no sun,
looking for food the foxes they run.
As the world turns from night to day,
but the shadows do not fade away.
The morning light brings colours in the sky,
as orange and red clouds go flowing by.
The wonders of the world we do not see,
the wonders that are around you and me.

The wind that moves through the trees,
the early morning winters breeze.
The start of a cold and fresh day,
with winter snow on it's way.
The weather outside is freezing cold,
it could be a killer to the frail and old.
Wrapped up in a blanket keeping warm,
seeking protection from the coming storm.
As the day goes on the heat will rise,
from the earth towards the sky.
Forming clouds of rain and snow,
how this happens I really do not know.
But it is all part of the pattern of life,
it is full of happiness and strife.

The winter nights and snow is in the air,
and the cold winter chill is everywhere.
As the snow falls silently to the ground,
and as it hits, it makes no sound.
But the wind that is howling by,
blowing the snow across the sky.
But the rain is also falling making sleet,
that would chill you from your head to your feet.
The trees are bare because the leaves have gone,
taken by the winter winds that get very strong.
The days are shorter then the days before,
and the nights get colder more and more.
All this happens as the world is asleep,
while the falling snow is becoming deep.

The winter wind blows across the winter sky,
the winter clouds are crying as they go by.
The temperature has dropped really low,
as the rain turns into ice and snow.
Bringing dangers to the left and the right,
as the winter snow falls on a winter's night.
As the snowfall covers every tree,
as the snow is carried on the breeze.
The temperature falls well below freezing,
in the very early hours of the morning.
The air is cold and it is clear,
creating frost everywhere.
The frost and the snow come together,
but this freeze will not last forever.
As the morning comes the temperature will rise,
as the sun rises into the winter skies.

The winter wind blows across the winter sky,
the winter clouds are crying as they go by.
The temperature has dropped really low,
as the rain turns into ice and snow.
Bringing dangers to the left and the right,
as the winter snow falls on a winter's night.
As the snowfall covers every tree,
as the snow is carried on the breeze.
The temperature falls well below freezing,
in the very early hours of the morning.
The air is cold and it is clear,
creating frost everywhere.
The frost and the snow come together,
but this freeze will not last forever.
As the morning comes the temperature will rise,
as the sun rises into the winter skies.

The winter wind blows across the winter sky,
the winter clouds are crying as they go by.
The temperature has dropped really low,
as the rain turns into ice and snow.
Bringing dangers to the left and the right,
as the winter snow falls on a winter's night.
As the snowfall covers every tree,
as the snow is carried on the breeze.
The temperature falls well below freezing,
in the very early hours of the morning.
The air is cold and it is clear,
creating frost everywhere.
The frost and the snow come together,
but this freeze will not last forever.
As the morning comes the temperature will rise,
as the sun rises into the winter skies.

The world is full of suffering and pain,
enough to drive everybody insane,
But there is an angel showing you wrong from right,
watching over you everyday and every night.
Showing you the path you should walk,
and telling you the words you should talk.
Trying to ensure you do not go astray,
so you can make it to Heaven one day.
But there is a demon out to get you,
telling you the wrong things to do.
Leading you to a place very hot,
where poor souls will eventually rot.
Partying everyday until you lose yourself,
and let's not talk about your sinking health.
Listening to the angel or the demon's voice,
is up to you because it is your choice.

Edward Wilson

The world is getting smaller as the nations grow,
where will this growth stop no one really knows.
People are reaching out into space seeking new lands,
not only humans reaching out but also the orang-utans.
Before humans leave earth, they send orang-utans,
the effect space has on humans they do not understand.
Orang-utans have already left the jungle and walk among us,
with proper disguises they do not cause any fuss.
They get jobs in health and safety and drives cars,
from the jungle to here they have come very far.
Learning to use a knife and a fork,
pretending to read and learning to talk.
Leaving the trees and the hot jungle nights,
on taking over this planet they set their sight.
Not planet of the ape but of the orang-utan,
this will be more then this human can stand.

The world outside is dark and grey,
but will it be like this through the day.
The clouds are gathering and it may rain,
down the streets and down the drain.
As the wind blows in from the west,
the world at this moment is at rest.
Because the world is resting in the morning dark,
as darkness rests on the streets and the parks.
As the streetlight prepare to show the way,
shining bright until the light of day.
Dancing in the wind the trees sway,
through the night and into the day.
The moonlight looks toward the ground,
as the wind makes it's howling sound.
All this goes on throughout the night,
but it also happens in the daylight.

There is a light outside my window that is shining bright,
and this light is lighting up a cold and lonely night.
Filling every corner of my dark bedroom,
shining in the corners and filling the gloom.
Where does this light come from and why is it here,
and why in the dark of the night this light is near.
I look around my bedroom and slowly towards the light,
but as I turn my head towards it, it vanishes into the night.
But I saw a light shining outside my window,
it was there and like a fire it did glow.
I was not dreaming of this I am sure,
so I may see this strange light some more.
So I will close my eyes and dream the night away,
and let my dreams carry me into a bright new day.
But in the daylight as the sun is shining on me,
I think about that light and what it may be.

There is a nasty odour moving through this place,
it has a ponytail, a name and a face.
It conducts itself like a nasty rat,
but it is really an unwashed tomcat.
Looking to make friends with any loser,
and in times of trouble they come together.
He only grooms himself once a year,
and his foul odour follows him everywhere.
Trying to fit in with human beings,
but his own body he never cleans.
He makes excuses for the way he is,
but if water falls on him, he will fizz.
His skin is dark, but is it ground in dirt,
using soap and water would really hurt.
His clothing get washed once a year,
on others do you think that this is fair?
Having to put up with an unfriendly smell,
that comes from the tomcat from hell.

Edward Wilson

There is some thing in the fog, there is some thing in the night,
will it get stronger or will it fade in the morning light.
There is some thing that is moving on the wind,
and the cold wind blowing is not very kind.
There is some thing that walks into your dreams at night,
and it is still there as you daydream in the daylight.
The things that hold you in your mind,
they are not nasty and they are not kind.
The things in our mind, the things that we put there,
keep us company in a world that does not care.
So the things that help us through the night,
are the things that haunt us in the daylight.

These feeling that I have are sinking fast,
holding on to love that can not last.
Going to places where I should not be,
trying to find the happiness inside of me.
Feeling the loneliness in my heart,
I think that we will be better off apart.
You run hot then you run cold,
as you have my heart in this frozen hold.
Our ship is sinking beneath the sea,
and there is no life jacket for you or me.
If we bail out now that will be the end,
no more lovers, no more friends.
But if we hold together through the storm,
and as life gets cold, we keep each other warm.
We may just make it to the end,
and remain lovers and remain friends.

This is the morning that I saw you, for who you are,
a low life rodent that plans to go very far.
You took my money and hang me out to dry,
while giving the eye to any female passing by.
I see all this but I am afraid to say,
because I am hoping that you will stay.
I know your behaviour is like a back alley rat,
but your roommate is a smelly tomcat.
Who also wants to get his purrs on me,
get away tomcat and leave me be.
But you come sniffing around my draws,
given the chance, you will do much more.
You are not number one but number two,
in reality only the tomcat really wants you.

This is the time and this is the place,
the first time that I saw your face.
No longer just a voice on the telephone,
now that I have found you, no longer alone.
You are a dream that slowly walks,
you are a vision that softly talks.
I have travelled through time to find you,
to find a love that will always be true.
A love that will be with me for all my life,
now I have found you, please be my wife.
So we can travel through time, you and me,
enjoying each other and all that we can see.
Travelling together into eternity,
travelling together you and me.

Edward Wilson

This time in the morning as I lay next to you.
observing everything that you say and do.
You are sleeping so I listen to the noises you make,
I will lay here silently, so you will not awake.
The wind blow gently against the window pane,
as softly from Heaven comes the gentle rain.
The birds are not singing as the morning starts,
but as the day goes on I am sure they will do their part.
But through all this you are still fast asleep,
as the morning sky continues to weep.
So I will lay here silently with the love of my life,
listening to the snoring noises of my wife.

Three days of fishing to find the truth,
that will make me happy or hit the roof.
Lies that are going are going around my head,
not only what I see but also what is said.
Feelings of doubt coming from every side,
so I bury my head so that I can hide.
But my backside is still up in the air,
troubles are still hitting me, but from where?
I close my eyes and I try to pretend,
that my broken heart is on the mend.
Never trying to look beyond my nose,
to see who is beating me with an emotional hose.
Never stopping to get my wish,
so for these three days I will fish.

Time waits for no one as time moves on,
one moment it is here and then it is gone.
Time seems to moves at the same pace,
it is we humans that against time we race.
It took millions of years for us to evolve,
from ape to man, or so we are told.
But there are humans that behave like orang-utans,
tree dwelling primates pretending to be man.
One such person I know quiet well,
but from looking at him it is hard to tell.
It is not that he scrapes his knuckles against the floor,
or that he enjoys swinging through trees more.
It is not that he is King Kong's son,
or he rolls around naked in the sun.
I just can not put my finger on it,
but from his behaviour, it seems to fit.

To kill a vision or to kill a dream,
is not as easy as it may first seem.
To take the hope of one man,
will take more then you understand.
To take love from someone's heart,
means tearing someone's world apart.
These things are not easy to do,
to destroy another was never a part of you.
You were born from love or lust,
you were not created to live as dust.
You were created to have love for each other,
and not to show hatred towards one another.
This is what we were created to do,
but to walk this path is up to you.

Edward Wilson

Trees of plenty in which I can play,
lazily sleeping the daylight hours away.
Roaming the rubbish bin for something to eat,
looking for something nice and sweet.
Trying to find something smelling worst then me,
something that is decomposing naturally.
Something that will knock me off my feet,
a maggot ridden piece of rotting meat.
That is a pure pleasure to my eyes,
with a smell that leaves me hypnotised.
Then find a blocked drain from which to drink,
it is a blissful aroma that does not stink.
As my afters I will try to find a juicy rat,
and that is dinner for this hungry tomcat.

Trick or treat it is that time of year,
the time that all children love to fear.
When ghost fly all through the night,
and fade before the early morning light.
A night full of monsters everywhere,
children wearing masks to hide their fear.
The true meaning is lost to time,
but it is not about candy you will find.
Wearing masks to hide, that part is true,
maybe you are hiding from the beast inside you.
With scary movies on television all night,
just buy some popcorn and stay out of sight.
So enjoy a movie, then again two,
and remain calm is what you should do.

Walking home as the sun is sinking low,
as the wind is blowing very soft and slow.
Blowing my body odour up the street,
from the top of my head down to my feet.
People rushing to get out of the way,
of an odour that get worst each day.
No deodorant can ever tame me,
as my body odour roams free.
The windows in the area all close tight,
as my body odour fills the night.
As a dark mist leaving his armpits,
and toxic bodily fluid he spits.
Melting the pavement and the ground,
killing the grass that is all around.
Finding a tree to sleep in for the night,
rest my tomcat until daylight.

Wallowing in the rubbish to improve my smell,
and when I get you in my sights, I will ring your bell.
I know that I am just a tomcat and I am aiming high,
I want to rock your universe and fill you sky.
With my special perfume essence of tomcat,
it will thrill you my darling and make you shed fat.
You are darling doggy with your hairy back,
and I will see that there is nothing that you lack.
I give you my heart of a silver platter,
in my world it is you that only matters.
Essence of tomcat a perfume I designed for you,
for you my doggy there is nothing I will not do.
Doggy do not change but stay as you are,
along this road together we will travel far.
A tomcat and his doggy hand in hand,
and we can live of the fat of the land.
You will never worry about what to eat,
as long as I am here to protect you my sweet.
I will feed you with fish tails and pedigree chum,
even my cockroaches, I will give you some.
Until I die and my body odour fades away,
I will never leave you until that day.

Edward Wilson

Watch me as I swing through the trees,
swinging so fast that I create a breeze.
Looking for a victim, some fresh meat,
someone new that I can finally meet.
Someone that is younger then me,
someone that will finally set me free.
I am an orang-utan with one desire,
to learn the secret of making fire.
Then I can stand up on two legs with pride,
as my true identity I will hide.
Pretending to be human is where I am at,
but most humans behave like large rats.
Is this a leap backward or a step forward,
I think being human would be good.
Giving up my title as a jungle VIP,
no longer swinging through the tees.
Getting out from under the shadow of King Kong,
leaving my daddy, now that would be wrong.
So I will stay here where I am a king,
and I will stop all this foolish thinking.
To forget about creating fire,
now swinging in trees is my only desire.

Weather swinging through the racking or in a tree,
as an orang-utan it is all the same to me.
Swinging on high seeking out my prey,
spotting a dog, now I will make her day.
chasing her into the canteen where she will play,
with a tomcat for the rest of that day.
But I am King Louie and I will wait,
but when the time is right I will not hesitate.
I will rush in with my animal charm,
and wrap her in my hairy arms.
realising that she has more hair then me,
I understand whatever will be will be.
I will take her to my dwelling,
which is up there in the racking.
If she is afraid of heights, I will knock it on the head,
because before our love starts, it is already dead.

What would you leave behind when you die,
will it be based on the truth or on a lie?
What mark on the world would you make?
would it be done in truth or just a fake?
How will the world remember you?
by something that you are going to do.
Or by something that you may say,
that may echo in the future day be day.
Again I ask because I do not know,
will I be a hero or a puppet show?
I ask myself this question everyday,
how will I be remembered when I go away.
I have plans how to leave my mark,
be a shining light in the dark.
To these plans I will try to be true,

White clouds gather in a night blue sky,
will it rain today or will it be dry.
The wind is blowing the clouds around,
the wind also is blowing leaves on the ground.
No birds are singing and I do not know why,
or why they are not flying in the sky.
The world is spinning and night turns to day,
as the daytime activities get under way.
The daylight hours are filled with movement,
as if it was a gift that is Heaven sent.
Flowers open as they start to bloom,
and daylight fills all the rooms.
Coming in through the windows,
and all the beauty of the daylight shows.

Edward Wilson

Winter is here and the nights are cold,
it helps to have someone to hold.
The leaves are falling from the trees,
carried away by the winter breeze.
The night is longer then it was before,
as the night time hours seem to be more.
In the early hours of the morning,
the world takes it time in dawning.
But it will happen just like the day before,
as the sun slowly rises once more.
The daylight is here for a little while,
making little children want to smile.
They are going to school to see friends,
where their playing seems never to end.
But they will be home before it gets dark,
so there will be no playing football in the park.

Winter is on its way and the nights are cold,
as the cold winter winds take a firm hold.
The leaves are being blown from the trees,
being carried away by the winter breeze.
The air is crisp also the air is clear,
because the winter months are here.
The snow is falling from the sky,
as the winter cloud float gently by.
Rain is falling and the ground is wet,
as the rain falls, there is no need to fret.
It will rain for a season also snow,
turning the world as white as snow.
Hiding the evil in a sheet of white,
covering good and evil in the same light.
But the cover of white is not true,
to do good or evil is up to you.

With no sign of life between your ears,
your eyes are open but you are unaware.
Doing two things at once is beyond you,
you have no idea what you are to do.
You have a brain but no instructions with it,
when you shake your head it rattles and does nor fit.
So it seems your brain is too small for your head,
thinking for yourself is something you dread.
No intelligence just a bad singing voice,
staying away from you is my only choice.
You are not really ugly, but somewhat thick,
and your singing really makes me sick.
But that's alright, what more can I say,
you will find an idiot to love you one day.

With no sign of life between your ears,
your eyes are open but you are unaware.
Doing two things at once is beyond you,
you have no idea what you are to do.
You have a brain but no instructions with it,
when you shake your head it rattles and does nor fit.
So it seems your brain is too small for your head,
thinking for yourself is something you dread.
No intelligence just a bad singing voice,
staying away from you is my only choice.
You are not really ugly, but somewhat thick,
and your singing really makes me sick.
But that's alright, what more can I say,
you will find an idiot to love you one day.

Edward Wilson

You are a cheat and I do not know how,
but you behave like you are an over weight cow.
You swing your handbag on the street corner,
not happy with one so you look for another.
The more the mariner is what you do,
the local bicycle and people ride you.
Down the road and alone the lane,
and round the corner once again.
Treated like a baby to this very day,
you can not keep yourself at bay.
You lack the control of a human being,
your personal belongs in the dustbin.
But you try to convince others, who you are,
making out that you are a shining star.
But you are a rat from the drains,
swinging your handbag over again.

You are a little bundle of great joy,
you make me feel like a little boy.
You are older then me by a couple of years,
I want to stare your happiness and your fears.
You do not know what you do to me,
and I do not know what you see.
When you look at me with those eyes,
that somehow leave me hypnotised.
You bring me happiness whenever you are near,
your mad little ways I always want to share.
Your crazy behaviour makes my heart sing,
because you are my everything.
You really are a dream come true,
these are the things that I think off you.

You are a nightmare and you really not there,
your life is smoky mirrors and you are not here.
You are an illusion of the worst kind,
as a parasite you rob people blind.
You hide your evil under the name of the Lord.
but you really have no interest in God.
You make noise like an empty drum,
your views are narrow and you seem dumb.
Your laziness is seriously very bad,
your attitude to life is really very sad.
You claim not to eat blood of any kind,
but plaint sap is pant blood you will find.
So vegetarians eat the blood of vegetables,
you do not accept this because you are not able.
Do you have a brain, I really do not know?
because no signs of intelligence do you show.

You are a tomcat living in the wild,
you never wash and that is your style.
You hiss at others every chance you get,
your memory is short, so you will forget.
To leave those alone that are better then you,
it happened before, so you already knew.
That these others can roar louder then you,
but like an idiot, you do what you do.
Rushing in like you were a big cat,
but you smell like a little rat.
Thinking that you what you are not,
because you are always smoking pot.
You need to focus and get yourself clean,
use some soap and water, know what I mean.
Attack your teeth with a toothbrush,
then from your breath, people won't rush.

Edward Wilson

You are an orang-utan who thinks that he is smarter then the rest,
because you can create fire, now you think that you are the best.
Your father King Kong would be very proud of you,
because you have achieved what do could not do.
You went further and you took a driving test,
an orang-utan behind the wheel of a car is a pest.
But you tried and tried again until you passed,
you were the first road legal orang-utan but not the last.
You got a work permit to work among the humans,
you shaved your face and on two feet you stand.
You form small words that passes for talking,
you wear back support so you are upright when walking.
You have tried to forget your past but you are wrong,
Remember little orang-utan you are the son of King Kong.

You are here in my head and in my heart,
you live behind my eyes when we are apart.
You share my dreams both night and day,
within my heart you will always stay.
You are the sunshine shining on me,
you are my light setting me free.
My heart melts as I touch your hand,
your power over me I do not understand.
But your love is everything that I need,
wherever you go I will follow your led.

You are my dream as I sleep at night,
you are my fantasy in the daylight.
You are the reason that I carry on,
the love in my heart for you is very strong.
Every beat of my heart calls to you,
to let you know that my love is true.
To have you in my arms to hold,
is worth more to me then gold.
You are my dream and you are my life,
you are my future and you are my wife.
So we will travel on through one life,
as we journey together as husband and wife.

You are my lady of the morning and my dreams at night,
you are the one that I wake up next to in the morning light.
You are future and my shelter in life's thunderstorm,
when I feel lost and alone, you keep me warm.
The feelings of love that you lock deep inside,
come to the surface as tenderness that can not hide.
Your face as you sleep looking so heavenly,
sometimes I can not believe that you are next to me.
But I know that I will love you for the rest of my life,
and take care of you forever my darling wife.

Edward Wilson

You are my love and all I hold dear,
and I dream each night of holding you near.
Holding you in my arms and in my heart,
your face is behind my eyelids when we are apart.
Feelings of love and calm wash over me,
and the spirit of your love sets me free.
We will live in each other's hearts,
no matter how far we are apart.
We are together staring the same space,
and behind my eyelids I see your face.
Each time I close my eyes you are there,
so I know that in my heart you live there.
You are the one that holds my life together,
with all my heart I will love you forever.

You are the centre of my world and you live in my head,
it is your love that keeps me warm when I am in bed.
Wishing that I had you here in these arms of mine,
but I am here all alone in a world so unkind.
Living in the closed space inside my heart,
a place where we can be together and never part.
This is the dream that I hold on tight too,
because every dream I have is about you.
So I listen to the strong wind as it blows,
having a love in my heart that no one knows.
It seems a little strange the way this has turned out,
but you are my secret lover that makes my heart shout.

You are the dream that I have at night,
you watch over me until daylight.
You walk with me in my heart,
so we are never truly apart.
When I feel I am alone you hold my hand,
when I feel sad; by my side you stand.
You live behind the lids of my eyes,
you tell me the truth and never lie.
You are with me wherever I go,
you are my love come rain or snow.
These feelings that I have each day,
means that I love you in a special way.
I will love you for the rest of my life,
you are my future and you are my wife.

You are very small also beautiful too,
I feel happy whenever I am near you.
Your personality is that of a child,
you make me laugh with your style.
Five foot noting with curly hair,
and those silly moments what we share.
You do not walk but you glide,
as I hide my feeling deep inside.
The feeling I have for mad little you,
means that I like being near to you.
You are as mad as the day you were born,
bringing a little happiness a life that is torn.
So I take my hat off to you with no regret,
to a dear friend that I will never forget.

Edward Wilson

You deserve each other you really do,
you are a lying two faced cheat too.
He will take your money and disappear,
you take peoples hearts and do not care.
He treats you like the child that you are,
you break hearts and leave a scar.
He has another woman besides you,
you don't want to accept that this is true.
You have his lies in your heart to keep,
your eyes are open but you are asleep.
Like Southampton he plays at a dell,
he is playing extra time again, oh well.
He like football, but he loves to fish,
playing at Southampton is his next wish.
So you deserve each other, you really do,
he is just as under handed as you.

You have your beard cut and shaved,
but you never washed, is this how you behave?
You are two tones, one dark and the other light,
from where your clothes block the sunlight.
Cleanliness is next to Godliness, so they say,
so please try to use soap and water everyday.
At least once a week, try to wash your hair,
because you have lice and fleas living there.
Washing away the smell harder then you think,
in a nutshell, man you really truly stink.
Your breath is like a blazing fire,
off old burning plastic burning higher.
You truly are unaware that you stink,
women love you or so you think.
So take the hint you smelly old man,
women run from you whenever they can.

You lay there in the morning with your tail between your legs,
with deep sorrow and regret running through your head.
You sold your kennel and gave the money away,
to someone that you hoped would love you one day.
But he was in love with your money from the start,
he always had planned to break your heart.
People washed their hands in forgetting you,
when you gave up your kennel for something new.
Now your hair needs grooming, you need someone to care,
because your love and your money is no longer there.
So howling at the moon is what you will do,
crying your life away is all that is left for you.

You live in my dreams and you live in my life,
you are my everything and you are my wife.
You are my sheltr in a world gone mad,
you make me happy when I am feeling sad.
You are the one that cares for me,
and I will love you for all eturnity.
You watch over me as I sleep,
and your love I will always keep.
Every moment that I am with you,
is like one hundred dreams come true.
So I hold you forever in my heart,
a love without end, a love without start.

Edward Wilson

You look like a zombie, who has just woken up,
you have the brainpower of a helpless pup.
Your work mates are just as useless as you,
sharing a brain cell is what the three of you do.
Three of a kind displaying one damaged brain,
your behaviour is far beyond insane.
The three are just like puppets on a string,
if that is so, who is doing all the pulling?
Off the strings that control all of you,
by yourself there is nothing you can do.
So the three of you operate as one,
like a child that is playing in the sun.

You make noise like an empty tin can,
you seem like you are a hollow man.
You have no life that you live,
you have no love that you can give.
Your world is empty just like you,
living a lie you are never true.
The lies that you create is a bottomless pit,
and you have fallen into the middle of it.
You claim intelligence but you are not,
you are a fool who thinks he is hot.
Dragging other's into your personal hell,
with all the rubbish and lies that you tell.
But your make believe world is closing in,
as your lies have started crumbling.
But you will tell more lies to cover a new crack,
but your lies no longer cover you back.
So you back yourself in a corner and reload,
unaware of all the lies you have already told.

You promised to love me forever and a day,
but now you want me to just go away.
If I sold my house, you would look after me,
and we will live in your flat happily.
But you took all the money to pay your bills,
and you treated me like I was a cheap frill.
I feel that you do not love me anymore,
you have changed from how you were before.
I sold my house and the money was fine,
but you took all my money and left me behind.
Things were good until the money ran out,
now all we do is scream and shout.
If I had listened to those around me,
I would still be happy and I would be free.
But instead I am tied down to a rat,
who is sharing his flat with a tomcat.

You seem to control me in my sleep,
you use me and leave me in a heap.
I seem to be your puppet on a string,
and I have lost control of everything.
I stand there in the night crying in the rain,
I have lost control and I am going insane.
Looking for a way out of this,
to find my way back to happiness.
Do you realise what you are putting me through?
and all these things that you make me do.
one hour with you seems like many more,
each more painful that the hour before.
Release me from these chains and set me free,
and prove to me that you really do love me.

Edward Wilson

You touch my heart when you touch my hand,
these feelings confuse me and I do not understand.
Do I love you and is this dream for real,
or is it just confusion that my heart feels.
I look into your eyes as you look at me,
and I ask myself what is it that you see.
Because the things that I see when I look at you,
are the things that can make my dreams come true.
But the situation is not perfect at all,
the higher I get the further the fall.
I may love you but you belong to another,
so we can only be friends and not lovers.
So I will watch you from afar and smile in my heart,
because I know that we will always be apart.

You were made in darkness of a jackal and a snake,
your existence on earth is not a mistake.
You are the son of satan born in hell,
after your father satan from Heaven fell.
You try to led the innocent astray,
as you pray to your father satan each day.
You hold your false church gathering new souls,
dragging them to hell is your one true goal.
You live in the darkness but you appear in the light,
when all is said and done you are a child of the night.

Your breathing is toxic stripping paint from a wall,
you are an ecosystem and that is not all.
This condition came from years of neglect,
and your shin fizzes whenever it gets wet.
Your hair is home to birds, rats and mice,
not to mention the different kinds of lice.
Flies always rush to get away from you,
please take it personal, it is because of you.
Are you black or are you white,
it is hard to tell at first sight.
I know you are strong, I can smell you,
use some soap and water please will you.
People tell you but you do not take the hint,
you think your body odour smells like mint.
Flowers wilt and die when you are near,
you are an ecological time bomb, this is clear.

Your face in the morning as you gently sleep,
I offend wonder off the secrets that you keep.
You look so peaceful with your hair lying on your face,
and I know that here by your side will always be my place.
Your soft and gently body laying on the bed,
with loving dreams going through your head.
The clock ticks as the time passes constantly by,
whenever we are together time seems to fly.
I listen to you sleeping late at night,
and I see you sleeping in the daylight.
You are my little piggy and my life,
to you my darling and loving wife.

Edward Wilson

Your face is like the sea after a storm,
your eyes are deep, gentle and warm.
Your smile is like a summer's day,
taking all my heartache and pain away.
Your breath is like the ocean breeze,
your touch brings me to my knees.
You are my everything; you are my life,
you are my heartbeat; you are my wife.
All the little things that you do,
makes my love stronger for you.
The way you glide as you walk,
your gentle whispers as you talk.
Every moment with you is a dream come true,
for the rest of my life I will love you.

Printed in the United States
By Bookmasters